Laurence Hutton

From the Books of Laurence Hutton

Laurence Hutton

From the Books of Laurence Hutton

ISBN/EAN: 9783743324169

Manufactured in Europe, USA, Canada, Australia, Japa

Cover: Foto ©Thomas Meinert / pixelio.de

Manufactured and distributed by brebook publishing software (www.brebook.com)

Laurence Hutton

From the Books of Laurence Hutton

Lawrence Sutton

FROM
THE BOOKS OF

LAURENCE HUTTON

"The dainties that are bred in a book"

NEW YORK
HARPER AND BROTHERS
MDCCCXCII

Copyright, 1892, by HARPER & BROTHERS.

All rights reserved.

TO

CHARLES B. FOOTE
AND
BEVERLY CHEW

BOOK LOVERS BOTH

THIS BOOK ABOUT BOOKS

PREFACE

FROM THE BOOKS OF my own library, comfortably rich in the literature of the seventeenth and the eighteenth centuries, I have gathered these oddities and curiosities of Books. The chapters upon "Some American Bookplates," and upon "Grangerism and the Grangerites," were published originally in the *Bookbuyer;* the chapter upon "The Portraits of Mary Queen of Scots" appeared in the *Century Magazine;* the chapters upon "Portrait Inscriptions," and upon "Poetical Inscriptions," were printed in *Harper's Bazar;* and the chapter upon "Poetical Dedications" first saw the light in the *Princeton Review.* They have, all of them, been revised, and some of them have been rewritten; and they contain not a little additional matter gathered from the desultory reading of later years.

In the quotations, both in prose and in verse, the original spelling has been retained as far as possible. The Index is made for the benefit of all Bookmen ; and the absolutely blank leaves disconnecting the various chapters, that each may be separately extra-illustrated, is a concession to what is considered the depraved taste of the Grangerites.

The little volume, as it here appears, is inscribed not only to the Book-knower who is more familiar with every branch of my subject than I can pretend to be, but to the Book-lover who may care, perhaps, to glean from its pages certain odd and curious facts concerning the dainties that are bred in Books.

LAURENCE HUTTON.

CONTENTS

CHAP.		PAGE
I.	ON SOME AMERICAN BOOK-PLATES	3
II.	ON GRANGERISM AND THE GRANGERITES	33
III.	ON THE PORTRAITS OF MARY QUEEN OF SCOTS	59
IV.	ON SOME PORTRAIT INSCRIPTIONS	83
V.	ON POETICAL DEDICATIONS	131
VI.	ON POETICAL INSCRIPTIONS	155

ON SOME AMERICAN BOOK-PLATES

CHAPTER I

ON SOME AMERICAN BOOK-PLATES

HOW many book-buyers and book-lovers in this civilized country, and in this enlightened nineteenth century, have any knowledge of Book-plates? With boiler-plates, and butter-plates, and racing-plates, and fashion-plates the average reader is perfectly familiar; but Book-plate to him means nothing at all, or it means what it is not. Go to a large retail book-shop in any one of the leading American or British cities during the busy holiday season, and ask the frequenters what they know upon this subject. Nine hundred and ninety-nine out of every thousand never possessed a Book-plate; nine hundred and fifty have seen Book-plates, but do not know what they are; and nine hundred and twenty-seven never heard of Book-plates at all. Yet Book-plates are almost as old as the printing of books; and the production of them, at one time, was nearly as common as the manufacture of the volumes they marked.

Book-plates are not the engraved plates which are used in the illustrating of books, nor are they the stereotyped plates from which books are printed; they are the engraved or printed labels, of any form or design, which, pasted in the inside of the front covers of books, serve to denote the ownership thereof. They vary greatly in style, according to the period to which they belong, or to the taste or social position of their possessors; from the fantastic and primitive designs of Albert Dürer to the graceful and artistic examples of Abbey or Bracquemond; from the elaborate quarterings of an hundred coats-of-arms in the volumes of Vere de Vere, to the simple JOHN FISKE in the tomes of the author of "The Outlines of Cosmic Philosophy."

The term Book-plate is awkward, and confusing to the uninitiated. It originated in England in the middle of the eighteenth century, and has since been used generally by English-speaking peoples. The Latin *Ex Libris* ("From The Books Of"), still employed by the French and other Latin races of the Continent, is much more happy. Etymologists and linguists may perhaps find traces of it in the literal translations so often to be seen in the limited private educational libraries of both sides the Atlantic at the present day. *Ex Libris Gulielmi Stubbsi* is unquestionably the parent of "Bill Stubbs, One of his Books."

The earliest Book-plate known to collectors is German, and is believed to belong to the later years of the fifteenth century. The oldest *dated* Book-plate, also German, contains the figures 1516; and a number of highly-prized specimens bear the well-known initials "A. D.," but unfortunately no date. They were designed, although, as it is believed, not etched or engraved, by Albert Dürer (1471-1528), who is called "the Father of Bookplates."

But few English Book-plates which are

earlier than the Restoration are said to exist. The oldest known example, bearing an engraved date, is of the year 1574; and William Marshall, so prolific in frontispieces of English books during a great part of the seventeenth century, is the first English artist who is known to have signed a Book-plate, and that in 1662. Other specimens of early English Bookplates contain the signatures of such well-known artists as George Vertue (1684–1756), Hogarth (1697–1764), Bartolozzi (1730–1813), and Thomas Bewick (1753–1828).

The strange absence of these designating marks in England during the many years they are known to have been so common in other countries, is attributed to the fact that a great number of the more richly bound volumes in English libraries contained their owners' crests, stamped on the outside of the leather binding. The earliest English examples of these marks, whether within or without the covers, were simply coats-of-arms, with no mottoes or names. Only nobles or wealthy persons or corporations could own books at that period; and armorial bearings were considered a sufficient mark of proprietorship. They were, of course, familiar to all brother collectors, and at the same time they were more easily recognized and deciphered by the lower orders, who could not read written or printed words. These heraldic devices in a great many instances have been followed by later British bibliophiles. In France, on the other hand, we find bright and fantastic designs, plays upon proper names, ingenious monograms, drawings characteristic in some way of their owner's profession or position in life, all of them unconventional and imaginative, the French differing as greatly from their neighbors over the Channel in their Book-plates as in their art generally, or in their literature itself.

The earliest examples of American *Ex Libris*, like the English, are heraldic in style; but they are no more American than is the copy of the King James Bible or of the Book of Common Prayer, in the cover of which they found their way to New England or to the Carolinas from the Mother Country. Many of them, nevertheless, are of great interest now, and are as valuable in their way as are Knickerbocker knick-knacks or colonial chairs, because of their association with the famous families who made our early history for us, or their association with the Fathers of the Republic who fought for our rights to design our own Book-plates, and who gave us the glorious privilege, for so many years, of pirating the British books into which we put them.

Among the colonial Book-plates in possession of the collectors are those of the Washingtons, the Beverleys, the Lees, and the Byrds of Virginia; the Penns and Hopkinsons of Pennsylvania; the Vaughans and Pepperills of Maine; the Quincys, the Royals, the Olivers of Massachusetts; the Carrolls and Magills of Maryland; and the Schuylers, the Morrises, the Clintons, and the Livingstons of New York.

The most interesting American Bookplate to an American is, naturally, that of the Father of his Country. John and Andrew Washington arrived in Virginia in 1657, during the Protectorate, bringing with them, besides their principles and their integrity, the heraldic symbols of their family. Their crest gave us a national shield, and suggested our flag, while it has marked their books during several generations of Washingtons both in the Colonies and in the States. Some fifteen years ago a number of volumes were advertised for sale, and were sold, in Philadelphia, which purported to have belonged to the private library of General Washington at Mount Vernon; they all contained Book-plates, but it is believed that neither the Book-plates nor the books were genuine. They certainly did not possess the authenticated pedigree of the specimens now preserved in the Library of the Boston Athenæum and elsewhere.

That John Franklin, brother of Benjamin Franklin and son of a non-conformist tradesman in England, was entitled to bear the arms he engraved in his books is very doubtful; but there can be no question that the Washingtons and their social peers, north and south of the Potomac, had every right to the crests they used.

One of the earliest and most interesting of colonial Book-plates is that of "William Byrd, of Westover in Virginia, Esquire." The famous Westover Mansion, on the James River, about two hours' sail below Richmond, was for at least two generations of Byrds the vice-regal court of Virginia. It might have served as a model for that New Castlewood on the beautiful banks of the Potowmack, to which Colonel Esmond, of blessed memory, took his dear spouse in the reign of the first George, to pass the delightful Indian summer of their lives, thankful for its rest and sweet sunshine.

William Byrd, the earliest American of that name, came to this country in 1674, seventeen years after the arrival of the Washingtons, and fifty-six years before the immigration of the Esmonds. He inherited the estates from an uncle, and settled near the falls of the James River, on the site of the City of Richmond. The Westover Mansion was built a few years later.

William Byrd was barely of age when he left the Mother Country. He acquired great wealth as a planter and an Indian trader, and at the time of his death, and for many years previously, he was Receiver General of his Majesty's Revenues for the Colony. He was succeeded by his only son, the second William Byrd, who, like the Warringtons some generations later, was sent to England for his education. He was a student of the Middle Temple, a fellow of the Royal Society, and, according to the inscription on his monument at Westover, a man of great accomplishments, who "made a happy proficiency in light and varied learning," was "thrice appointed Publick Agent to the Court and Ministry of England," and "after being for thirty-seven years a member, at last became President of the Council of the Colony." He survived his father forty years. The third and last William Byrd, also a man of mark and influence in the Colony, is believed to have died soon after the outbreak of the Revolutionary War. The famous Westover Manuscripts, first published in 1841, were written from 1728 to 1736, by William Byrd, second.

The Byrd Book-plate is, unfortunately, unsigned and undated, but it probably belonged to the author of the Westover Manuscripts, and was engraved during his residence in London. Its owner, no doubt, ordered it in England upon the receipt of his appointment, carrying it and the books it marked, with the rest of his household goods, to the new country to which he had been sent. It is presumably older than the *Ex Libris* of " Robert Elliston, Gent. Comptrol^r of His Majestie's Customs of New York in America MDCCXXV.," which came into the possession of Mr. Richard C. Lichtenstein, of Boston, a few years ago, and is the earliest known heraldic American Bookplate bearing a date and the address of its owner. The engraving, which is purely Jacobean in style, is too fine, however, to have been done by any colonial artist as early as 1725.

The earliest distinctively American Book-plates are, naturally, those which are the work of the earliest American engravers—Hurd, Callender, Turner, Dawkins, Revere, Doolittle, the Mavericks, and Anderson. Of these, Nathaniel Hurd was not only the first, but the best. He was born in Boston in 1729. His father, also a native American, was a goldsmith in that city, and the younger Hurd was his apprentice, turning his attention particularly to engraving on copper. The first plate executed by him is believed by Mr. Lichtenstein—a recognized authority on such subjects—to have been the *Ex Libris* of Thomas Dering. It bears the initials NH, and was dated 1749, when the artist was barely out of his teens. Hurd was considered the foremost cutter of dies and seals on this continent, and for thirty years—he died in 1777—he engraved Book-plates for a great number of prominent families and societies throughout the Colonies, including those of Harvard College.

Henry Dawkins, an Englishman long resident here, engraved the Book-plate of John Burnet, of New York, signing it in full, and dating it 1754, five years after the Dering plate by Hurd. Of

Dawkins very little is known. He was originally a worker in metals, designing and moulding fancy buttons and the like in New York. Dr. Anderson told Dunlap that he remembered seeing ornamental shop-bills and "coats-of-arms for books," which Dawkins had engraved before the year 1775. But until recently, when Mr. Beverly Chew, of New York, discovered in a copy of Tonson's edition of Pope's Homer this *Ex Libris* of John Burnet, no trace of Dawkins had been found in this country earlier than 1760, when he signed the frontispiece of a Collection of Psalms, Tunes, etc., published in Philadelphia a year later. The natural supposition now is that the Book-plate was engraved in Philadelphia or New York. A writer in the *Magazine of American History* speaks of Dawkins as having been arrested for counterfeiting in 1776, and of his petition to be hung rather than suffer the long confinement to which he was sentenced. Whether he was hanged, imprisoned, or pardoned is not recorded.

The second native American engraver was Paul Revere (1735-1818). A number of his Book-plates are familiar to collectors, and are as rare and as valuable as is the "Landing of British Troops" or "Boston Massacre" (1770), by which he is known to those of his fellow-countrymen who know that he was an engraver at all. He was apprenticed to a goldsmith, and, without a master, he learned the art of engraving on copper. As an enthusiastic and ever-active patriot, the work in which he took the greatest pride, no doubt, was the paper money of the Commonwealth of Massachusetts (1775). This he designed, engraved, and printed; constructing with his own hands the primitive press from which it was issued. He was the typical Yankee boy, who, before he's sent to school, well knows the mysteries of that magic tool, the pocket-knife, and who, before he dies, not only makes the machine, but makes the machine that makes it.

That art in this country is in its infancy is proved by the fact that a contemporary of the earliest of the American engravers lived to see the work of the men of the present day, and to compete with it ; that the father of wood-engraving in America laid down his tools less than a quarter of a century ago. Alexander Anderson was born in the City of New York in 1775. When a lad of twelve he made his first attempt at his art with a graver which he had fashioned out of the back-spring of his old penknife, and on a copperplate rolled out of the pennies given him to buy a new one. At the age of fourteen he was apprenticed to a physician; he studied medicine for five years, and was licensed to practice in 1795. But the passion for engraving was too strong to be resisted, and all his leisure time was devoted to it. He supplied the newspapers with the small figures of houses, ships, mechanics' arms, and runaway negroes, cut on type-metal, with which they illustrated their columns of wants, when Washington was President, and James Duane or Richard Varick was Mayor of New York; and twenty-five years before the death of Paul Revere, Anderson was a professional engraver, and a ripe and good one. In 1793, when employed in copying drawings on wood after Bewick for an American edition of "The Looking Glass," he discarded the type-metal upon which he had been working through half the volume, cut the rest of the illustrations upon boxwood, with tools of his own invention and construction; and signing his name to the first wood-cut published on this continent, he gained for himself the title of the American Bewick.

Anderson continued in the daily practice of his profession almost up to the time of his death, at a great age, in 1870; and until Abel Bowen began to engrave upon wood in Boston in 1812, he had no competitor in this country in that branch of his art. He illustrated many books of all classes—a catalogue of which has lately been printed by Mr. Charles C. Moreau, of New York, for private circulation—and he made a number of Book-plates, including his own and one of Columbia College.

Doolittle (1754-1832) and the Mavericks began their professional lives not much earlier than Anderson, but they ended them almost half a century before he cut his last block. Doolittle was a native of Connecticut, self-taught, and the author of a copperplate view of "The Battle of Lexington," engraved from a drawing by an eye-witness, and published, with other plates of like character, in New Haven in 1775. These were believed for some time to have been the earliest specimens of engraving of historical subjects executed in America. Paul Revere antedated him, however, by several years.

Peter R. Maverick (1755-1807), called Peter Maverick the first, and his son Peter Maverick (1780-1831), etched and engraved in New York many Bookplates, which are highly prized by the collectors. The younger Maverick is best known as an engraver of bank-notes, and as the instructor of Asher B. Durand, who became his partner in 1817.

There is but a small band of collectors of Book-plates in the United States, and it is only within a few years that this harmless but interesting hobby-horse has been saddled and ridden here. The late James Eddy Mauran, of Newport, had thirty-five hundred examples of all nations and all ages, and Mr. Richard C.

Lichtenstein possesses upwards of three thousand — all of which were kindly placed at the disposal of the writer in the preparation of this chapter. Valuable and interesting as these are, they seem very meagre in quantity by the side of the twenty thousand specimens which Mr. J. J. Howard, of Dartmouth, near Blackheath, England, a founder of the Harleian Society, and editor of *Miscellanea Genealogica*, has gathered together during the last forty years.

Book-plates are valuable and interesting for a number of causes; on account of the artist who designed and engraved them, on account of their antiquity, their rarity, or on account of the personal qualities or position of the men and women whose books they mark. Plates that are signed, dated, or addressed are, of course, more interesting than those which have no such stamps; and of course the *Ex Libris* of a Daniel Webster, an Edward Everett, a William H. Prescott, or a Winfield Scott, is of more value than are those which are simply Book-plates and nothing more. All these Book-plates, too, are naturally of infinitely greater value in the books their owners read and loved, and in which their owners put them, than, when torn from their proper homes, they are gathered together in the asylum of a collector's album. Mr. Andrew Lang, in "The Library," says that any one of twenty coats-of-arms on leather is worth one hundred times the value of the volume which the leather covers. If this be true, and it *is* true, of the personal marks on the outsides of books, it is certainly quite as true of the marks within. There are many editions and many copies of the poems of Jean Ingelow, and the *Ex Libris* of Charlotte Cushman is not at all uncommon, but Miss Cushman's own copy of Jean Ingelow, containing Miss Cushman's Book-plate, is worth, for Miss Cushman's sake, an entire edition of "The Old Days and the New," published after Miss Cushman's death, and to be bought now for a few shillings.

Miss Cushman is one of the few American women whose coat-of-arms, or whose name, is to be found upon American

Book-plates at the present time. To Mrs. Elizabeth Græm Ferguson belongs, it is said, the distinguished honor of having been the first of her sex on this continent to mark her books in this way. She was a lady of literary ambitions, who translated—but never published—"Telemachus" into blank verse before she was out of her teens, and who printed a number of original poems in the later years of her life. She was born in Philadelphia in 1739, and she died in the same city in 1801. No copy of her Book-plate, which was heraldic in design, is now known to the collectors; but she figures in Allibone's "Dictionary of Authors," and some specimens of her verse are to be found in Griswold's "Female Poets of America," in Duyckinck's "Cyclopædia," and in Stedman and Hutchinson's "Library of American Literature."

M. Poulet-Malassis, in *"Les Ex Libris Français"* (Paris, 1874), declares that "the eighteenth century was the golden era of Book-plates, the designs and the mottoes were so witty, so brilliant, so eccentric, and so varied." This may have been true of the *Ex Libris* of France, but it is hardly true of British and American Book-plates of the same period. It is only within a decade or two that the English-speaking bibliophiles have marked their books, to any extent, with other than heraldic symbols, and to such symbols, in many instances, the book-lovers on our side of the Atlantic had no right whatever. A well-known American family abandoned, not long ago, the crest which it had borne upon its silver, its carriages, and its books for four or five generations, upon discovering that it had sprung from a family whose crest was entirely different, or who had no crest at all. Nothing was needed by Hurd or by Maverick but a surname and a work on heraldry; the connection between the coat-of-arms and the man who bore the name being a matter of as much indifference to engraver and to purchaser then as it is, in their grandsons' time, to Tiffany and to Brentano. The Poulet-Malassis of a hundred years ago, on the other hand, no doubt, playing upon his own name, justified his descendant's claims for his variety, eccentricity, brilliancy, and wit by designing for himself an *Ex Libris* upon which was engraven an uneasy hen on an uncomfortable nest, and some punning motto, in choice old French, about "Foul Play," or "My pretty chickens and their dam."

This is hardly more fantastic or ingenious than is a well-known Book-plate of a much later date, on which the two towers of Notre Dame de Paris are made to form the initial capital H, while across the entire front of the cathedral are seen the letters U. G. O.; and over the top of all, in a flash of lightning, is engraven the legend "*Ex Libris* Victor Hugo." It is hardly possible to conceive of any of the British poets of a hundred years before Hugo's time, when the golden era of Book-plates existed in France, and the golden era of books existed in England, as indulging in an *Ex Libris* so eccentric, so brilliant, or so witty as this.

In marked contrast with the *Ex Libris* of the French poet is that of the American professor who is doctor as well as poet, and who has travelled, in his One

Hoss Shay, from the Atlantic to the far ends of the land, singing Songs of Many Seasons and in Many Keys, and carrying help and comfort to thousands of patients who never saw his face, but whose bruiséd hearts have blessed him, and still bless him, for their healing. The books in his library bear the image of "The Chambered Nautilus," that

> "Ship of pearl, which, poets feign,
>   Sails the unshadowed main,—
>   The venturous bark that flings
> On the sweet summer wind its purpled wings
> In gulfs enchanted, where the Siren sings,
>   And coral reefs lie bare,
>   Where the cold sea-maids rise to sun their streaming hair."

"If you will look into Roget's 'Bridgewater Treatise,'" said the Autocrat one morning, "you will find a figure of one of these shells and a section of it. The last will show you the series of enlarging compartments, successively dwelt in by the animal that inhabits the shell, which is built in a widening spiral. Can you find no lesson in this?"

> "Build thee more stately mansions, O my soul,
>   As the swift seasons roll!
>   Leave thy low-vaulted past!
> Let each new temple, nobler than the last,
> Shut thee from heaven with a dome more vast,
>   Till thou at length art free,
> Leaving thine outgrown shell by life's unresting sea."

George Bowland drew for the author of "The Poets of America" a Book-plate upon which is seen Pan piping with all his heart, in Syracusan times, and in haunts of shepherd, nymph, and satyr, the prelude of some pastoral ditty, to fauns who knew not Wall Street and nothing cared for trade or last quotations. The motto "Le Cœur au Métier" was suggested to Mr. Stedman by Mr. Matthew Arnold, who, in his address to the members of the Authors Club, in 1883, urged all men of letters, as well as all men of affairs, to put their hearts into their work. Of this Book-plate three sizes have been engraved; the smallest, covering hardly more space than a postage-stamp, fits beautifully in, and ornaments, the Elzevirs of the seventeenth century and the midget folios of this, which are among its owner's collection of precious books.

Mr. Aldrich's Book-plate contains a comic mask, surmounted by a black bird in the act of uttering sweet music, and it is intended, perhaps, to represent a Daw, and to be symbolic of Margery of that name. Mr. Lawrence Barrett's plate had the Mask of Tragedy on an open volume, with torch and dagger; and its motto was *Esto quod esse videris.* Mr. Booth's books are marked with a crest, and the motto, *Quod ero spero.*

Mr. Brander Matthews's Book-plate, designed by Mr. Edwin A. Abbey, is peculiarly fitting to an American, who is not only a collector of French dramatic literature and the author of the " Theatres of Paris " and of " French Dramatists of the Nineteenth Century," but is also the author and editor of books relating to the American stage, and the writer of American plays. It represents the aboriginal American's discovery of a Greek comic mask, and the legend, taken from Molière, asks him, " What think you of this comedy ?"

The variety and the ingenuity of the *Ex Libris* of the present day in this country are shown in these examples. Others are more fantastic, and all are intended to be symbolic of the profession or of the taste of the men to whom they belong. Mr. George W. Childs, of Philadelphia, places the pen where he thinks it should be, above the sword. Mr. Edward Eggleston selects a monk reading, with a nimbus and a star above his head, and this line in old English characters, "Flie fro' the presse and dwell with sothfastnesse;" and Mr. Dean Sage, an enthusiastic fisherman and collector of the literature of the gentle art he loves, puts into his copy of the "Treatyse of Fysshyinge with an Angle," or into his first edition of "The Complete Angler," that rod, that net, and that timorous trout, which, we are told, are the Contemplative Man's Recreation.

It may be remarked in passing that Book-plates in books do not always prove the ownership of the volumes which contain them. We have seen how the *Ex Libris* of Washington was forged; and it is said that a dealer in London to whom application was made for a specimen of the *Ex Libris* of David Garrick, confessed that he had none for sale, except in the books of Garrick's day, in which he (the dealer) had pasted them, finding, by so doing, that the books and Bookplates brought better prices! The collecting of *Ex Libris*, however, has preserved many interesting examples which would naturally, every year, be lost or destroyed in re-binding by ignorant workmen who have no knowledge of their value, or which are concealed and lost under later *Ex Libris* pasted above them.

And it must be confessed, in closing, that all collectors, no matter what they may collect, are in a measure destructionists, although they may claim that they destroy only to preserve. They have, sometimes, very little hesitation in burning scores of cottages for the sake of tasting the crackling on their special breed of little pigs; many priceless documents have been mutilated in order to obtain the easily duplicated signatures they contained; many unique books have been defaced for the sake of the not very rare portraits bound within them; or, to go back to the very beginning of "collecting" in this country, many valuable heads have been spoiled in order to gratify the enthusiastic hobby of our aboriginal collectors of scalps!

ON GRANGERISM AND THE GRANGERITES

CHAPTER II

ON GRANGERISM AND THE GRANGERITES

THAT a certain class of bibliomaniacs and bibliolaters should be denounced as biblioclasts and bibliophobians by all the great community of bibliocists, bibliophilists, bibliographers, bibliopolists, bibliologists, bibliopegists, bibliotaphists, bibliothecarys and bibliognostes would seem, to the lay mind, to imply a very serious condition of affairs. Yet this is, and has been, the position of the Grangerites since the founder of the sect published his great work, one hundred and twenty odd years ago.

James Granger (*cir.* 1716-1776) was Vicar of Shiplock, in Oxfordshire, and author of " A Biographical History of England from Elizabeth to the Revolution, Consisting of Characters Dispersed in Different Classes, and Adapted to a Methodical Catalogue of British Heads." It was "Intended as an Essay towards Reducing our Biography to a System; and a Help to the Knowledge of Portraits," etc., and it contained a preface showing the "Utility of a Collection of Engraved Portraits to Supply the Defect and Answer the Various Purposes of Medals." (London, 4°-1769.) To this was added, in 1806, by Mark Noble (1784-1827), rector of Barming, in Kent, "A Continuation of Granger's History, from the Revolution to the End of the Reign of George I.," the materials having been supplied from the manuscripts left by Mr. Granger and from the collection of the editor himself. The first edition of Granger's work (1769) was in two quarto volumes, each in two parts —hence the erroneous impression that it appeared in four volumes, as did the later editions, which were octavos. It was printed on one side of the page only, in order to facilitate the insertion of additional prints by the purchasers and subscribers; and it was introduced by a Dedicatory Epistle to Horatio Walpole,

Esquire; who, in return, after Granger's death, said, in print, that its author had drowned his taste for portraits in an ocean of biography; and that, although he began by elucidating prints, he at last sought portraits, only that he might write the lives of the men they represented. Which sounds very much like Mr. Walpole.

In 1773 Dr. Samuel Johnson, who did not realize how many of his own portraits would be known to the collectors of a century later, said: "Granger's 'Biographical History' is full of curious anecdotes, but might have been better done. The dog is a Whig. I do not like much to see a Whig in any dress, but I hate to see a Whig in a parson's gown." In 1776 Mr. Boswell, who certainly did not realize that his own great work would be looked upon within an hundred years simply as a magnificent omnibus, into which Mr. Granger's disciples would crowd all the men of Boswell's own day, wrote from Edinburgh to Bolt Court: "I have, since I saw you, read every word of Granger's 'Biographical History.' It has entertained me exceedingly, and I do not think him the *Whig* that you supposed. Horace Walpole's being his patron is, indeed, no good sign of his political principles."

Granger's History was the first book extended by the introduction of extra prints illustrative of its text; and Mr. Granger was the original Extra-illustrator, the father of the noble band of Grangerites. Unlike his descendants he wrote his book to illustrate his portraits; he did not collect his portraits to illustrate his book. He was followed at once by other collectors, who wanted a valid excuse for their collecting, and an asylum for their collections; and Clarendon's "History of the Rebellion and Civil War of England," Walton's "Lives," "The History of the Worthies of England, Endeavoured by Thomas Fuller, D.D.," John Aubrey's "Lives of Eminent Persons," and other contemporary historical and biographical works, were extended and enlarged; many lesser illustrated books suffering, naturally, for the benefit of these. Granger's collection of upwards of fourteen thousand portraits was sold after his death. A correspondent of the *Gentle-*

man's Magazine, for May, 1782, says that they were secured in one unbroken lot by Lord Mountstuart for £1500, but this was not the case. They were sold at auction by Mr. Greenwood in the Haymarket, April 6, 1778, and the following days, the catalogue describing them as " dating from the earliest specimens of engraving to the present time." Lord Mountstuart, afterwards first Marquis of Bute, was a patron of Granger, and he is mentioned by Boswell in the letter to Johnson quoted above (August 30, 1776), as being anxious to find a proper person to continue Granger's work, upon Granger's plan, offering to give such a person generous encouragement.

The most cruel things that have ever been said about the Grangerites are to be found in " The Book Hunter." John Hill Burton (1809-1881) declared that the illustrator is the very Ishmaelite of collectors; his hand is against every man who loves books, and every book-lover's hand is against his. He destroys unknown quantities of books for the sake of enriching a single volume of his own with the portraits and other prints he finds in them; and what is worse, as he does not always make his ravages known, many a book is sold to the unwary person, who is ignorant of the damaged condition of his purchase. Mr. Burton could tell tales, he said, fitted to make the blood run cold in the veins of the sincere book hunter about the devastations of the Grangerites, who are in his eyes literary Attilas, the Genghis Khans of literary plunder and pillage, spreading ruin and terror around them; they are monsters—whether green-eyed or not he was not quite prepared to state—who do make the meat they feed upon, and becoming excited in their work, go on ever widening the circle of their purveyances, and opening new avenues towards the raw material on which they operate. Granger himself was conceded to have been an industrious and respectable compiler, however, and Mr. Burton hinted that he is not, perhaps, to be held responsible for all the harm done in his name. Dibdin also acquitted him of *malice prepense*, although he asserted that Granger's History was published in an evil hour.

It is a matter of some surprise that the Grangerites, suffering for so many years from the abuse heaped upon them, have said so little in their own defense. Even Mr. Tredwell, in his "Plea for Bibliomania," apologizes for, rather than defends, the seductive art of privately illustrating books; and confesses his own sins in cutting up a new garment, like the old lady in the fable, to mend an old one; forgetting that it is often possible and justifiable to restore old and treasured gowns and jackets with pieces taken from some new raiment which is hardly worth the making up, and certainly is not worth the wearing out. An honest patch is better than shoddy at its best.

The Grangerites are, by no means, the only biblioclasts, nor the most persistent, nor the most ruthless. Mr. William Blades enumerated among "The Enemies of Books" (Trübner & Co., London, 1880), fire, water, gas, heat, dust, neglect, book-worms, and other vermin, and even book-binders and collectors! An extra inserted print of man, or beast, or house, or town, or field, or plain, does not always mean the destruction or mutilation of some valuable volume which once contained it. It indicates, simply, the survival of what in that book was most fit to be retained. In very many volumes which come from the printer's hands the illustrations are the best part, not infrequently the only part of any worth whatever. Thousands of ephemeral books and pamphlets have contained portraits of some "worthy," or views of some old theatre, or long demolished church, or palace, or public building, which tell better the story of their originals than all that their contemporaries ever wrote concerning them; and, except for these prints, the appearance of these originals would be as much a matter of uncertainty now, and quite as incomprehensible, as is the art of a dead actor or the habits of the dodo. They were not saved to posterity by the books in which they were bound, but by the collectors and the Extra-illustrators who realized their worth, and who plucked them from the burning, or from the rag and bottle shop. Brandy peaches are not so good, perhaps, as ripe peaches, but they are better than dried peaches, or than no peaches at all; and they are available and valuable when fresh peaches cannot be obtained. On the shelves of the closets of hundreds of enthusiastic collectors of jam are jars of Clingstones and Morris Whites, which would have comforted and refreshed no man if they had been left to rot upon the trees on which they grew.

Jonathan Richardson (1665-1745) graphically described a portrait as "a general history of the life of the person it represents; not only to him who is acquainted with it, but to many others who, upon occasion of seeing it, are frequently told of what is most material concerning him or his general character, at least; the face and the figure is also described, and as much of the character as appears by these, which oftentimes is here seen in a very great degree."

The earliest Grangerites were collectors of personal portraits only — of portraits proper, as the word is now understood; for in its primeval period all painting, whether of landscape or figure, was called portraiture. The Pre-Raphaelites painted a portrait of a mountain, a mill, and a man, the mill sometimes being as big as the mountain and the man often covering more space than the mill — and all on one panel. The first human likeness, according to Pliny, was drawn in Greece, and the original artist was a Corinthian maiden, who, with the charred end of a stick, traced the profile of her lover on the white wall, upon which, from the light of her lamp, his shadow was cast. The early Roman warriors had their own portraits painted upon their shields; and in the days of the Republic none but those Romans whose forefathers had attained dignity in the state, or who themselves had worn the purple, were permitted to sit for their pictures at all.

With engraved, etched, and printed portraits alone, of course, the Grangerites deal; and these go back only to the end of the fifteenth century, the earliest being from the gravers of Dürer and his contemporaries. The first English engraved portrait, according to Vertue, was that of

Archbishop Parker, by R. Hogenberg, and it is dated 1572-73. The earliest attempt at a collection of engraved portraits in one volume in England, according to Walpole, was Holland's "Heroölogia Anglicana," folio, London, 1620; which even in Walpole's day was very rare. It was suggested to its publisher by a Flemish work of the same character printed two years previously.

One of the earliest collectors of prints in England and one of the most enthusiastic, was John Evelyn, whose learned essays on Engravers and Engravings, brought down to his own times, are delightful and instructive reading to all collectors in ours. In 1690 he wrote to Pepys — a brother collector, and a quondam pupil of his in that respect — a long letter full of good advice as to what to buy and where to buy it, closing as follows: "I send you, sir, my face, such as it was of yore, but is now no more, *tanto mutata;* and with it what you may find harder to procure, the Earl of Nottingham, Lord High Admiral, which though it makes a gap in my poor collection, to which it was glad, I most cheerfully bestow upon you." Very rarely, indeed, in the history of man does one find such an instance of warm friendship as this, and it may be urged against Evelyn on this account, that he could not have been a collector in the proper sense of the word. A collector can exchange, but like the Old Guard he never surrenders; and he will not make a gap in his own lot to please any man who ever lived. Pepys himself, long before this time, was an enthusiast on the subject of portraits; and in his Diary he records more than once his purchases and the pleasure they gave him. He even sent commissions to the dealers in Paris; for on January 25, 1668, his wife "showed him many excellent prints, Nanteuil's and others, which at his desire had been brought to him out of France, of the king, of Colbert, and others, most excellent, and to his great content." There is no record of his having made any gaps in his collection, however, to enrich the collection of anybody else. Of course, neither Evelyn, nor Pepys, nor their contemporaries were Grangerites. The name and the genus had not then been invented. They had no thought of the Extra-illustration of books, but bought their prints for the prints' own sake, and from the natural collecting instinct of man, who is a collecting animal.

Of the art of collecting, and of the charm of collecting, much has been written, and much has been said, but nothing more keenly appreciative or more valuably instructive than the words of love and wisdom which Richard Marriot, in St. Dunstan's Church-yard, in Fleet Street, printed in 1653 for the dear old linen-draper of Chancery Lane, who was a collector of Trouts in the Tamesis and the Lea.

Your complete angler for prints is not the man who fishes in preserved waters, with priced-catalogues for fishing lines, and long bank-accounts for hooks; nor is he the man who sends his agents to fish for him, as the Japanese have their dancing done, by proxy; nor yet the superannuated angler, with gouty foot on chair, who bobs for gold-fish in a tub in his own dining-room, like the familiar man after the old painting; but, like Izaak Walton, he is the modest, humble piscator, who trudges many a weary but happy mile for his simple luncheon of speckled beauties which will hardly weigh two to the pound avoirdupois, but who feels that he has well earned them before he lands them, and who enjoys them all the more because he has, perhaps, neglected the mixing of his daily bread in the making of his flies or the digging of his worms. With great delight he studies the winds and the clouds, the proper seasons of the year, and the proper times of the day, and decides whether he shall try a red fly or a dun fly or the humble bait that turns. Long experience has made him familiar with the habits and haunts of the prints he fishes for, and well he knows, and dearly he loves, the quiet pools, so near the rapid waters of Broadway, the Strand, or the Quai d'Orsay, where the fat ones lurk waiting to be caught by the angler who knows how to strike them, and how to play them, and how to keep them when he gets them in.

There are collectors and collectors, however. Some gather prints for the sake of the artist who engraved them, seeking, for instance, nothing but the works of Hollar and Vertue, and everything of Vertue's and Hollar's that their purses will buy. Others collect only for the sake of a subject—Bonaparte, Shakspere, Washington, Mary Stuart, London, Steamships, or Cats; securing every portrait or view of their subject, good, bad, indifferent, authentic or ideal, natural or artificial, possible, probable, and absurd; while others, collecting to illustrate a certain book, or books, gather pictures of every person, or place, or thing upon which the text touches. There are, also, specialists in style; collectors of first impressions, or of artists' proofs only; collectors who will accept nothing but line-engravings, mezzotints, or etchings, who draw the line at woodcuts; and there are omnivorous collectors who draw the line at nothing but a photograph, who accept everything that is a picture, from a Bartolozzi and a Blake down to the commonest stamps on the meanest handbills which come from the press. These plebeian collections are, in certain respects, the most valuable of all. They contain the rank-and-file of life, of topography, and of architecture, subjects which are too humble to attract the attention of the great artist, and are only to be found embalmed in the columns of some illustrated daily, weekly, or monthly journal, but which go to make history, and are not to be ignored because they are mere "process-pictures" of no artistic worth. These common cuts, too, often preserve the portrait of some person or place of no little importance, which by accident of time or opportunity have no other or no better representation. The Extra-illustrators of Ireland's "Records of the New York Stage" will look in vain, outside of an old number of "Frank Leslie's Lady's Magazine," or of "The Memoirs of Lester Wallack," for a portrait of Mrs. Hoey, to make their book complete; while inserted in different copies of Dr. Francis's "Old New York" are newspaper cuts of many interesting historical old buildings, which would never have been reproduced at all if some special artist on the spot had not had the rare good-luck to find them next door to a fire on the one side of them, or to a murder done on the other.

Grangerism is thus defined by the author of "The Book Hunter":—"Illustrating a volume consists in inserting in, or binding up with it, portraits, landscapes, and other works of art bearing a reference to its contents;" and the Arch-Enemy of the sect, parodying Dibdin's famous "Recipe for Illustration," contained in "The Bibliomania," and itself bordering on the satirical, proceeded to show how a devotee of what he calls the peculiar practice would naturally go to work to illustrate that piece of English verse which begins:

> "How doth the little busy bee
> Improve each shining hour."

Dibdin's example is a paragraph from the works of Speed, the historian. But as Speed is not always accessible, and as Dr. Watts's familiar poem is not altogether adaptable, the Neophyte for whom this particular chapter is written—it is respectfully inscribed to the Virtuoso who is more familiar with the subject than the writer can pretend to be;—the Neophyte will take, for instance, this chapter itself, and turning back to the opening paragraph he will make, at random, a list of names found in the text, including, among others, those of James Granger, Thomas F. Dibdin, Dr. John W. Francis, Mr. Joseph N. Ireland, John Hill Burton, James Boswell of Auchinleck, Samuel Johnson, and Mary Stuart.

Armed with this list he will at once set himself out to procure every portrait of these personages he can buy, beg, or exchange, no matter at what period of life it is taken, by what class of artist it is executed, or to what process of engraving it belongs. And this pursuit, if properly carried out, he will find a liberal education in itself.

To begin at the foundation of his subject, he will discover, probably, but one portrait of Granger, and that not very easily. He will see that the first edition of Granger's "History of Engraved British Heads" contained no specimen of the Engraved British Head of its author, but that a vignette from the hand of C.

Bretherton is to be found in the edition of 1775, and that this print itself is now very scarce.

Dibdin's picture will not be so far out of his reach. He was painted by T. Phillips, R.A., and engraved by James Thomson for the edition of "The Bibliomania" published in 1840. Besides this there are several privately engraved plates. Of Dr. John W. Francis there are at least four portraits within the collector's reach; the familiar head by Julius Hollman serving as a frontispiece to "Old New York;" a portrait by the same artist contained in "The Knickerbocker Gallery;" a three-quarter length by Herring in "The National Portrait Gallery" (Philadelphia, 1836); and an uncommon print, folio size, published by the Appletons. Two portraits of Mr. Joseph N. Ireland, author of "The Records of the New York Stage," are in existence: one etched by H. B. Hall in 1869, and a second engraved by J. C. Buttre in 1884.

Of John Hill Burton there is no likeness in the early edition of "The Book Hunter," although a "Nook in the Authors' Library," and a full-length portrait by W. B. Hole were given in the *Édition de luxe* printed in 1883.

If the Laird of Auchinleck—pronounced Affléck—had come into the world without the enthusiasm, the impudence, the curiosity, and the untiring want of tact which distinguished him, he might have gone down unhonored into the dust from whence he sprung, and have died entirely undrawn except by some Ayrshire limner of no repute. But as the friend and biographer of Johnson, he became so famous that his portrait by Reynolds had been engraved no less than ten times when the first edition of Croker, and the eleventh of Boswell, appeared in 1831; and how often it has been copied since no man can tell. This picture by Sir Joshua, the full-length portrait by George Langton, an engraving of which, by E. Finden, was published by Murray in 1835, and the grotesque head in profile by Lawrence, are the best known portraits that have come down to us.

The print bearing the legend, "James Boswell, in the Dress of an Armed Corsican Chief, as he appeared at Shakspere's Jubilee at Stratford-on-Avon, September, 1769," is curious and rare, and was, no doubt, originally published with his concurrence. It speaks for itself, and for Boswell!

Concerning the portraits of Dr. Johnson alone, many pages might be written. His face is as familiar to-day as is that of Bonaparte, Shakspere, or Mary Queen of Scots. In one private collection of Johnson there are one hundred and fifty-three prints, no two of which are alike; and this collection is known to be incomplete. When the Neophyte comes to this name on his list he will be at a loss where to begin and how soon to stop. He will certainly be tempted to gather as many as his purse will buy.

The earliest authentic portrait of the great lexicographer is a miniature, the painter of which is unknown. It belonged to Mrs. Johnson, and was first engraved in 1831 by Finden, for the earliest edtion of Croker.

In 1756 Sir Joshua Reynolds painted Johnson in three-quarter length, seated in an arm-chair at a table, and with pen in hand. This has been repeatedly engraved, although the most rare prints are the work of J. Heath (quarto), for the first edition of Boswell, 1791, and that of J. Baker (octavo) for the edition of 1793. Another portrait by Reynolds was without a wig and with the hands raised. It was executed about 1770, and went into the collection of the Duke of Sutherland. A third by the same artist bears date 1773. It has the left hand on the waistcoat button, and was painted for Bennet Langton. In 1778 Reynolds painted his friend again, this time "a kit-kat," and for Mr. Malone. It represents its subject as near-sighted and holding a book close to the eyes, a portrait which Johnson resented as an unfriendly act on the part of the painter in handing down to posterity the inflictions and infirmities of the original. These have all been painted in replica; and more than once, and scores of times, have they been engraved. Sir Joshua's hypothetical "portrait" of Johnson as he was supposed to have looked when a child of two years, preternaturally heavy in head, and already with deliberation and pedantic care engraven on his front, is described by Mr. Tom Taylor in his "Life of Reynolds" as beautiful in color and in fine preservation.

Johnson was painted by Barry—full face and finished only as far as the shoulders—about 1781. Opie's portrait, a three-quarter face turned to the left, was engraved by J. Heath for the folio dictionary of 1786. Miss Reynolds, a niece of Sir Joshua, painted a miniature on ivory, as well as a three-quarter length, life-size portrait on canvas, which latter her sitter himself described as "Johnson's grimly ghost." Of the last portrait, by Trotter, Johnson said: "Well, thou art an ugly fellow! But still I believe thou art like the original!"

Besides all these, mentioned briefly above, the collector will find prints of Johnson in all conditions, of all sizes, and by engravers good and bad, after original portraits by Northcote, Zoffany, Humphrey, Harding, and others, as well as engravings of the bust by Nollekens, and the statue by Bacon in St. Paul's Cathedral.

Here, taken almost at random, are but a very few examples of the pictures the Extra-illustrator will hunt for, and perhaps find, in Extra-illustrating a few stray pages upon Extra-illustration. But they will whet his appetite for more. He will have spent a few dollars—well invested—and many happy days in making his collection; and he will spend happy nights in arranging and counting and admiring it. Those portraits which have margins too large he will cut down to fit, those which are too small he will have "backed" and "inlaid" by Trent, Lawrence, or Toedtberg, or if he be an artist as well as an enthusiast, like Mr. Moreau, he will inlay his own prints.

When these are bound in with the text, and with, perhaps, a few autographs added, the Grangerite has made for himself an absolutely unique book, into which he has put so much of himself that his Extra-illustrated copy becomes part of himself, and a joy to him forever. And he blesses himself that he has a hobby; while he blesses Granger for giving his hobby a reason and a name.

ON THE PORTRAITS OF MARY QUEEN OF SCOTS

CHAPTER III

ON THE PORTRAITS OF MARY QUEEN OF SCOTS

THE question of the personal appearance of the last Queen of the Scots is a matter of as much uncertainty to-day as is the greater question of her moral character. Scores of volumes have been written to prove her virtue or to proclaim her infamy, and hundreds of artists have endeavored to picture the face, a glimpse of which, it was said, would move even her enemies to forget her follies and forgive her faults. That she was the most beautiful princess, if not the most beautiful woman, of her time, tradition and history have declared for three hundred years; but wherein lay her loveliness of person, or how far, as a woman, she was worthy of respect, neither history nor art can positively assert. The subject of her portraiture, therefore, merits a chapter to itself.

Horace Walpole, author of "Anecdotes of Painting," and no mean authority upon the subject, to which he had given close attention, said in a letter to Sir Joseph Banks, first published in George Chalmers's "Life of Mary Queen of Scots" (1822), that he could never ascertain the authenticity and originality of any of the so-called portraits of her, except that one which was in the possession of the Earl of Morton. "It agrees," he wrote, "with the figure on the tomb at Westminster; in both the nose rises a little towards the top, bends rather inward at the bottom, but it is true that the profile on her medal is rather full, too. Yet I should think that Lord Morton's portrait and the tomb are most to be depended on."

The picture known as the "Morton Portrait" was painted, according to generally accepted tradition, by Mary's own order in 1567, when the unfortunate Queen was twenty-five years of age, and during the first year of her confinement at Loch

Leven. It is on a panel, is of life-size, and has been attributed to Lucas de Heere. The present Earl of Morton is descended from Sir William Douglas, Laird of Loch Leven, and the elder brother of George Douglas, to whom Mary is said to have presented the picture, because of his assistance in effecting her escape from the castle. The fact that it has been in the possession of this family for upward of three centuries is its strongest claim to originality. It has frequently been engraved.

The full-length, life-size, recumbent effigy in alabaster on the tomb in Westminster Abbey was placed there upon the removal of the remains of Mary from Peterborough in 1612. Its costume resembles in many respects that of the Morton portrait, by which perhaps it was suggested. The name of the designer of this monument has never been clearly ascertained, although it would appear from certain of the records kept during the reign of the first Stuart king of England that "Cornelius Cure, Master-Mason to his Highness's Works," did receive, during the years 1606 and 1607, various sums of money "for the framing, making, erecting, and finishing of a tomb for Queen Mary, late Queen of Scotland . . . according to a Plot thereof drawn"; and that "William Cure, his Majesty's Master-Mason, son and executor under Cornelius Cure," was paid other various sums in 1610, and again in 1613, for "making the Tomb to his Majesty's Dearest Mother."

From these it would appear that the monument was begun six years before, and finished one year after, the final interment, in 1612. John de Critz, mentioned by Meres in his "Wit's Commonwealth" (1598), as "famous for his painting," is generally believed to have been the architect of the tomb to Elizabeth in the adjoining chapel; and as they are similar in design and of about the same date, it is not improbable that he was the author of the "Plot thereof drawn" for the tomb to Mary. The figure, at all events, was executed less than a quarter of a century after Mary's death, and when there must have been many persons living in Great Britain who remembered her. Its correctness as a portrait does not seem to have been questioned then, and there is every reason to believe, with Walpole, that it is one of the best likenesses of her which has been handed down to us.

Without doubt the first attempt at portraiture of the Queen of Scots was made in her earliest infancy, for her little face was engraved upon the half-pennies issued from the Royal Scottish Mint at the time of her coronation in 1543, and when she was but nine months old. A number of these small coins are still preserved, and it is said that the name "bawbee," or baby, was originally given to that denomination of money because of its bearing the image and superscription of the Baby Queen. As a likeness, of course, this is of little value. Nor can much more credit be attached to the portrait of the bright, piquant little girl in the collection of Lord Napier, notwithstanding the fact that it bears a memorandum in the handwriting of Francis, seventh Lord Napier, dated 1790, to the effect that "this picture of Mary Queen of Scots, supposed to have been painted when she was about twelve years of age, has ever been considered to be an original picture, and has been in the possession of the Napier family for many generations." It is on canvas, two feet three inches high, one foot ten inches wide ; the complexion is fair, the hair light brown, the roses in the head-dress are crimson, and the gown is red, with white stripes. It resembles so strongly in face and costume, however, a portrait in the collection of the Earl of Denbigh, which is known to be that of an Infanta of Spain, who lived many years after Mary's time, and who was even suggested as a proper wife for her grandson, Charles I., that there can be little ground for the belief that it was intended for the Queen of Scots at all.

The earliest painted portraits of Mary are probably those executed in France before her marriage to the Dauphin in 1558, for it is an established fact that François Clouet, otherwise Jehannet or Janet, who was court painter successively to Francis I., Henry II., Francis II., Charles IX., and Henry III., made a portrait of her about the year 1555, which was sent to the Queen-

Regent of Scotland, Mary of Guise, but of which there is no trace now. In the collection of "Drawings of the Principal Personages of the Court of Henry II. of France," purchased by the Earl of Carlisle in Florence about an hundred years ago, and now at Castle Howard, there is a portrait of Mary ascribed to Janet, and, perhaps, the first sketch of the picture sent to her mother. It resembles the portrait in colored crayons in the library of St. Geneviève, in Paris, which has been reproduced by engraving in P. G. J. Neil's "Portraits des Personages Français," although they both suggest a woman of twenty or more, rather than a child of thirteen, and neither of them resembles in any way the subject of the Napier portrait described above. In the crayon drawing the eyes and hair are light brown.

Janet is known to have painted another portrait of Mary during her first widowhood, and when she was known as "La Reine Blanche," and the picture now at Hampton Court is believed to be the original of this. It is faded, and has every appearance of having been retouched and restored. It certainly belonged to Charles I., for it bears his monogram, "C. R.," surmounted by a crown, and has attached to it a note by the keeper of the king's pictures testifying that "it is Queen Marye of Scotland, appointed by His Majesty for the Cabinet Room, 1631. By Janet." Its history before it came into the possession of Charles has never been traced to the satisfaction of the antiquaries. The eyes are dark brown, the widow's white cap pressing on the forehead is opened at the sides to show the dark brown hair and joins a veil which passes around the cheeks and conceals the ears. The face is that of a decidedly elderly woman; and the expression is very sad. If by Janet, and of Mary, it could only have been painted when the Queen was in her nineteenth or twentieth year. An old copy of it is in the National Portrait Gallery at South Kensington, whence it was taken from the British Museum some years ago; and several pictures of the same type are to be found at Versailles and elsewhere.

Patrick Fraser-Tytler, the historian of

Scotland, published in 1845, for private circulation only, a monograph in which he attempted to prove that the picture now known as the "Fraser-Tytler Portrait" was the identical likeness painted in 1560 shortly before the death of Francis II., and sent by Mary, through Lord Seton, to Elizabeth. It belonged to an artist named Stewart, was bought by Fraser-Tytler from a dealer, and is now the property of the trustees of South Kensington. It is three feet one and a half inches long, and two feet three inches wide. The painter is unknown, although it has been ascribed to Zuccaro, who was only a lad during Mary's residence at the French court, and who did not go to Paris until the reign of Charles IX., ten or twelve years after Mary's return to Scotland. It is hardly probable that she sat to Zuccaro at any time. His only visit to England was during her long captivity, and when she was kept under the closest surveillance. Walpole believed that Zuccaro could never have seen her, and Labanof included him in a long list of artists who painted purely imaginative portraits of her, or who, for various reasons, could never have been the authors of the pictures of her which have since been attributed to them. The portrait of Mary and James VI., on one canvas, ascribed to Zuccaro, now in the Drapers' Hall, London, must of necessity be false as an historical if not as an artistic work; for the little prince, who was taken from his mother before he was a year old, never to see her again, is represented as a lad of five or six, standing by his mother's side. Curious stories are told of this painting, and of the manner of its coming into the possession of its present owners. There is a tradition that it was thrown over the walls of the Drapers' Garden for safety during the great fire by persons now unknown, and never reclaimed; another that Sir Anthony Babington left it with the Drapers' Company for safe-keeping, and could not get it back; still another that it was stolen from some of the royal palaces by Sir William Boreman in the reign of Charles II.; and it is even insinuated that it is a portrait of Lady Dulcibella Boreman, Sir

William's wife. It was cleaned at the instigation of Mr. Alderman Boydell towards the close of the last century, and it has been engraved by Bartolozzi.

Another portrait of Mary with a romantic history is that which was bequeathed by Elizabeth Curle, an attendant and faithful friend of the Queen, to the Scot's college at Douai, where it remained until the end of the French Revolution. During the Reign of Terror it was concealed by the priests of the college in the flue of a disused chimney, and it lay there, forgotten, for more than twenty years. It hung for some time after that on the walls of the Scottish Benedictine Convent at Paris, but in 1830 it was carried to the Roman Catholic establishment at Blair, near Aberdeen, where Agnes Strickland saw it, accepted its authenticity, and had it engraved as a frontispiece for one of her published works. The artist, as usual, is unknown, although it has been attributed, with slight authority, to Amyas Carwood, whose name appears upon the painting of the decapitated head of Mary which belonged to Sir

Walter Scott, and with which all visitors to Abbotsford are familiar. That the Curle portrait was a posthumous work there can be no question, as the scene of the execution is introduced in the background. A poor copy of it in her Majesty's collection at Windsor, is said by the different authorities to have been made in the reign of Charles I., of James II., and even as late as that of George III. Barbara and Elizabeth Curle were devoted servants of the Queen, and were present at the last scene of all at Fotheringay, in 1587. They escaped to the Continent with Gilbert Curle, the brother of Elizabeth and husband of Barbara, carrying the portrait with them, or, perhaps, painting it from memory during their exile. On the death of the last survivor of them it was left, as has been shown above, to the college at Douai. Their bodies were buried in the south transept of the church at Antwerp, which is dedicated to the patron saint of Scotland; and above the mural tablet erected to their memory, and supported by two carved angels, is a portrait of their Queen, copied—the head and bust only—

from the original work which they so dearly prized.

Still another picture of the Scottish Queen, with a strange, eventful history, is that which is known as the "Oxford Portrait" in the Bodleian Library. Sir David Wilkie discovered that there were two portraits of the same person—although unlike in costume and not very like in face—upon the same canvas; and after the outer picture had been carefully copied it was removed, leaving the portrait as the visitor to Oxford sees it to-day. The reason for painting this second picture over the first, and the period or the artist of either picture, no man now can tell.

The portrait of Queen Mary most familiar to the world, because most frequently reproduced, and upon which the popular idea of her personal appearance is based, is that known as the "Orkney Portrait," belonging to the Duke of Sutherland. Its painter is also unknown. The nearly effaced date, 1556, and the name Farini, or Furini, are said to be visible upon it; but it bears every evidence of being much more modern than the middle of the sixteenth century. It is said to have belonged to Robert Stuart, one of the many natural sons of James V. who fretted Mary's reign, and who was created Earl of Orkney by James VI. How this picture came into his possession tradition does not say. A well-known copy of it by Watson Gordon hangs in Queen Mary's room in the Castle of Edinburgh.

An interesting miniature of the Scottish Queen is now in America. As it has never been engraved or publicly exhibited, it is little known to collectors. It represents her at half length. The dress is black, trimmed around the neck, the arms, and upon the bosom with eider-down. Between the large ruff of the down about her neck, and the neck itself, is a fine, upright collar of stiff lace. On the head, and falling back over the neck, is a black velvet coif. The hair is what is called "Titian gold." The background of the picture is dark blue, and contains the legend, "*Maria. Regina. Scotorum.*" In the case of polished wood which holds it is a gold plate with the following inscription: "This original portrait of Queen Mary Stuart is an heirloom in the family of the Setons of Parbroath—now of New York—into whose possession it came through their ancestor, David Seton of Parbroath, who was Comptroller of the Scottish Revenue from 1589 to 1595, and a loyal adherent of his unfortunate Sovereign. It was brought to America in 1763 by William Seton, Esquire, representative of the Parbroath branch of the ancient and illustrious family of the forfeited Earls of Winton." There is a tradition that this picture was the gift of the Queen to her faithful servant, David Seton, who, although a member of the Kirk of Scotland, was never counted among her personal foes. A copy of it was presented by the late William Seton in 1855 to Prince Labanof, who believed it to be from life, and surmised that it was taken during her captivity. The face is beautiful but no longer young.

Of the very many other existing portraits of Mary, or of their claims to authenticity, it is hardly possible or necessary to speak here. Nearly fifty paintings of all sizes, generally believed to be "originals" by their owners, were exhibited at Peterborough, at the Tercentenary of Queen Mary's death, in 1887, and hundreds of engraved portraits, no two of which are exactly alike, are in the different private collections on both sides of the Atlantic, nearly all of which may be marked "doubtful." Vertue himself confessed that he did not believe "the fine head in a black hat, by Isaac Oliver, in the king's collection," which he engraved, to be a portrait of Mary, and he also questioned the authenticity of the picture known as the "Carleton Portrait," which he engraved for Lord Burleigh. Holbein died before he could possibly have painted Mary; Vandyck was not born until twelve years after her execution; Paris Bordone may have seen her, although there is no certainty of his having been in Paris after the reign of Francis I.; Zuccaro probably did not paint her, and yet to all of these artists "original" portraits are positively ascribed.

It is a remarkable fact that the more

beautiful is the face which is painted or engraved the less reason is there for believing it to be the face of Mary. A glance at the fullest collection of "Mariana," in which are prints good and bad, authentic, posthumous, apocryphal, ancient, and modern, will convince the observer that no woman, no matter how varied her expression, could possibly have looked like them all. The coins and medals struck during her lifetime to commemorate interesting events in her career, and still in existence in France and in Great Britain, so far as that style of portraiture is to be depended upon, may give a better and more reliable idea of her face in profile than any of the paintings which vary so much in expression and in color. Her head is to be found upon Scottish silver coins of 1553 and 1561, and upon a Scottish gold coin of 1555. There is a cast of a medallion at South Kensington, by Jacopo Primevra, which is very clear; and the medals containing her head and that of the Dauphin, which were struck in honor of their marriage, are still to be seen in their original state at Versailles and in other French galleries; but how correct any of these may be as portraits, it is not possible now to say.

After careful inspection of all the so-called "original portraits" of Mary Stuart, and after conscientious reading of much of the voluminous literature, contemporaneous and otherwise, in which she figures, it is not possible to accept any picture of her, either by painter or by writer, as absolutely correct. While the lock of her hair, found in a cabinet which was inherited by Charles I. from his father and is carefully preserved by the present Queen, "is of the loveliest golden hue and very fine," Nicholas Whyte, Burleigh's emissary, wrote to his chief in 1569, on the strength of information received from Mary's attendants, that her hair was "black or almost so." In the "Fraser-Tytler Portrait" the face is pale, the eyebrows of a pale yellow tint, the hair yellow rather than brown, and the eyes blue. In the picture supposed to have been presented by Mary to the Earl of Cassillis, one of the Scottish commissioners sent to act as a witness at her marriage to the

Dauphin, the hair is of a rich chestnut tint, almost black, the eyes and eyebrows are dark, and the complexion is that of a delicate brunette. In a miniature, dated 1579, with the monogram "M. R." in the corner, and sold in the Neville Holt collection in 1848 as "a reliable, original portrait of Mary Stuart," the hair is brown and the eyes gray. Janet painted her with light brown eyes and hair. Melville, in comparing the rival queens, said that Elizabeth's hair was more red than yellow, while Mary's was "light auburn, her eyes of chestnut color." Winkfield, an eye-witness of Mary's execution, described her eyes as hazel. Ledyard, in one of his poems, spoke of her *yeux un peu brunets;* and they all seem to agree that she had a slight but perceptible squint.

That Mary wore false hair, and of many different colors, there is every reason to believe. Elizabeth is known to have had a collection of eighty wigs, and her dear cousin, with the unusual advantages of so many seasons in Paris, is not likely to have been far behind her. Among the statements of the accounts of her personal expenditure are numerous items of *perruques de cheveux*, and Sir Francis Knollis, writing to Burleigh of the ever faithful " Mistress Mary Seton, the finest busker, that is to say the finest dresser of a woman's head of hair that is to be seen in any country," said, " And among the pretty devices she did set such a curled hair upon the Queen, that was said to be perewyke that shewed very delicately. And every other day she hath a new device of head-dressing, without any cost, and yet setting forth a woman gaylie well." This variety and eccentricity of coiffure naturally adds to the confusion, and makes greater the difficulty in identifying positively any of the portraits or descriptions of Mary. Historians say that her mother was tall and beautiful, that her father was dignified, having a fair complexion and light hair; and other and contemporaneous historians say that she inherited most of the characteristics of her parents, " being about the ordinary size, with fair complexion and Grecian features, and a nose somewhat longer than a painter would care to perpetuate; . . . her face was oval, her forehead high and fine." Froude, in later days, pictures her as graceful alike in person and in intellect, and as possessing that peculiar beauty in which the form is lost in the expression, and which every painter has represented differently; and Brantôme, one of the ancient chroniclers, summing it all up in one fine sentence, described her at her marriage to the Dauphin as being "more beauteous and charming than a celestial goddess."

"An angel is like you, Kate; and you are like an angel," was a very pretty speech for Shakspere's Henry V. to make to the French king's daughter, but it gives us of to-day no better notion of Katherine's beauty than do all the composite portraits, by painters and historians, of the wondrous loveliness of the Queen of the Scots.

ON SOME PORTRAIT INSCRIP-
TIONS

CHAPTER IV

ON SOME PORTRAIT INSCRIPTIONS

NEXT to the familiar lines, beginning, "Good Frend for Jesu's Sake Forbear," carved upon the stone which covers the supposed grave of Shakspere, in the chancel of the church at Stratford, no verses of any kind relating to Shakspere are more familiar to the general reader of English literature than are those written by Ben Jonson, and prefixed to the famous Droeshout portrait of Shakspere, contained in the Four Folios of his Plays:

"This Figure, that thou here seest put,
It was for gentle Shakespeare cut;
Wherein the Grauer had a strife
With Nature, to out-doo the life:
O, could he but have drawne his wit
As well in brasse, as he hath hit

> His face; the Print would then surpasse
> All, that was ever writ in brasse.
> But, since he cannot, Reader, looke
> Not on his Picture, but his Booke.
>
> "B. I."

This poetical effusion has served to establish in a great many minds, and despite all sorts of contradictory statements, the conviction that Shakspere lived, and had a being, and even that he wrote, and was portrayed by limners; and it seems to prove that Jonson knew him, and believed in him, and that Jonson believed, as well, in the Droeshout portrait. It is unquestionably one of the most important of the Portrait Inscriptions which have come down to us from the seventeenth century; but that it is only one of very many similar dedicatory stanzas, is probably a fact of which the general reader is not aware. A number of these, including one to Jonson himself, were seen in the Exhibition of Engraved Portraits made by the members of the Grolier Club of New York in December, 1891; and in the collection of Mr. Beverly Chew — kindly placed at the disposal of the writer of this chapter — are some two hundred examples of this species of English verse, all of them curious and some of them rare, while a few, signed by their authors, are nowhere to be found among the fugitive pieces in these authors' collected works.

Concerning the Droeshout portrait of Shakspere innumerable papers, pamphlets, and even books, have been written. It is found in all sorts of conditions or "states," no two of which are absolutely alike; and the first "state" is, naturally, the best. Of this only one example is known to exist, a proof, which belonged to Mr. Halliwell-Phillips. It was on the exceedingly rare title-page printed before the word "*coppies*" was corrected to the single "*p*" of the rare First Folio; and all later impressions are believed to have been printed from a re-touched plate.

The name Droeshout was spelled by his contemporaries, and perhaps by himself, in a number of ways — Droeshout, Droshaut, Drossaert, Drussoit, etc.

The Droeshouts were a Netherlandish family of artists who settled in England during the last quarter of the sixteenth century. The first of the name of whom there is any record was " John, a painter." Michael, who is believed to have been a son of John, is described "as a graver in copper, which he learned in Brussels." Michael's son, Martin, was baptized in the Dutch Church, Austin Friars, April 26, 1601, fifteen years before Shakspere's death. Another Martin, probably an uncle, figures in the records of the same church as "a painter, of Brabant." The younger Martin was admitted a member of the church in 1624, a year after the publication of the First Folio; and he is, in all probability, the author of the Shakspere portrait. His name also appears upon still existing engraved heads of James, Marquis of Hamilton, who died in 1625; George Villiers, Duke of Buckingham, assassinated in 1628; Sir Thomas Overbury (1581-1613); Dr. John Donne, engraved for "Death's Duell," published in London in 1632-33; George Chapman (1557-1634), etc.

The Droeshout print was placed upon the title-page of the First Folio, between the words of the actual title and the names of the printers—" Isaac Iaggard, and Ed. Blount, 1623"; and it bears the signature of the engraver in full. Jonson's lines were on the leaf facing the title-page, as was not infrequently the custom in those days. In the second issue of the Third Folio, 1664, the Droeshout print was removed from the title-page to make room for the enumeration of the seven doubtful plays, and was placed over Jonson's lines, so as to face the title, like the frontispieces of the present time.

Mr. George Scharf, Curator of the National Portrait Gallery in London, and a recognized authority upon the subject, in a long and exhaustive article upon "The Principal Portraits of Shakspere," contributed to *Notes and Queries*, for April 23, 1864 — Shakspere's birthday — expresses the opinion that the earliest impressions of the Droeshout print afford a very satisfactory indication of the individual appearance of the man, that the style of wearing the hair and the smooth, round cheeks accord with the monumental bust; and that the engraving, very probably, represents the subject as he appeared towards the close of his life. The plate is sharp and coarse, he continues, but there is very little to censure with respect to the actual drawing of the features; and he believes that Droeshout worked from a good original—some limning or crayon drawing, which having served its purpose became neglected, and is now lost. Alas, and alas, that this original limning—if it ever existed—exists no longer!

Malone, on the other hand, said that "there is no way of accounting for the great difference [in artistic skill] between the print [of Droeshout's Shakspere] and his spirited portraits of [Gen. William] Fairfax and Bishop Howson, but by supposing that the picture of Shakspere from which he copied it was a very coarse performance."

While Mr. Scharf thinks that the print exhibits Shakspere in the ordinary garments of a private gentleman of the period, other writers profess to believe that it represents him in the character of *Old Knowell*, in Jonson's "Every Man in His Humor," which tradition says Shakspere acted at the original production of the comedy in 1598; and this, perhaps, may account for the Laureate's enthusiastic indorsement of the portrait of the Player.

Mr. Scharf thinks, too, that the Droeshout head and stiff collar were followed by William Marshall in his small oval portrait of Shakspere which was prefixed to the 1640 edition of "The Poems." The body-dress and close-fitting sleeve are similar in point of construction; and while the embroidery is omitted altogether, the exact number of buttons is reproduced; the head, however, is looking the other way, the background is light, and the left hand holds a sprig of laurel. This portrait has also an inscription, to wit:

"This Shadowe is renowned Shakespear's, Soule of
    th' age,
The applause, delight, the wonder of the Stage,
Nature herself, was proud of his designes,
And joy'd to weare the dressing of his lines,
The learned will Confess, his works are such,
As neither man nor Muse can prayse to much.
    Forever live thy fame, the world to tell
    Thy like, no age shall ever paralell."

William Marshall engraved chiefly for

the booksellers, and he excelled in portraits. Some twenty-five examples of his work were in the Grolier Exhibition, including heads of Michael Drayton, 1637; Sir Thomas More, 1639; Sir Francis Bacon, with eight lines in Latin, 1640; Ben Jonson, 1640; James Shirley, with four Latin lines, 1646; and William Camden, 1652. Marshall was emphatically the medium for the expression of Portrait Inscriptions in English, and at this same Grolier Exhibition there were no less than six specimens of his work in that direction. Besides this inscription to Shakspere, there were Walton's lines to Doctor Donne, 1635; four lines to Francis Quarles, 1645; eight lines to Sir John Suckling, 1646; nine lines to John Fletcher, 1647; eight lines to Herrick, 1648; and Thomas May's lines to John Quarles, 1648.

Another evident copy of the Droeshout head is to be found in the 1655 edition of "Lucrece." It is the work of William Faithorne the elder, who was born in 1616—the year of Shakspere's death. It contains two lines of verse, but they refer to Lucrece and Tarquin, not to Shakspere himself.

Faithorne was a prolific engraver. He was a pupil of Hollar in England, and of Nanteuil in France; and he was well-known to Evelyn and Pepys, and to all the art-lovers of his day. Walpole said: "Faithorne now set up in a new shop at the Sign of the Ship, next to the Drake, opposite to the Palsgrave's Head, without Temple Bar, where he not only followed his art, but sold Italian, Dutch, and English prints, and worked for booksellers." Pepys wrote in his Diary, November 7, 1666: "Called at Faythorne's, to buy some prints for my wife to draw by this winter, and here did see my Lady Castlemaine's picture done by him from Lilly's, in red chalke and other colours, by which he hath cut it in copper, to be printed"; and on December 1st of the same year, the Diarist added: "By coach home, in the evening, calling at Faythorne's, buying three of my Lady Castlemaine's heads, printed this day, which indeed is, as to the head, I think, a very fine picture, and like her."

Thomas Flatman (1633-1688), who is described as having been skilled in painting, poetry, and law, paid to Faithorne, in the 1662 edition of Faithorne's "Book of Drawing, Etching and Graving," the following poetic tribute:

> "A '*Faithorne Sculpsit*' is a charm can save
> From dull oblivion and a gaping grave."

Although Flatman is generally forgotten at the present day, there are evidences that he was not entirely unknown to Alexander Pope a century and a half ago. The first edition of Flatman's Poems appeared in 1674, and contained the following lines:

> "When on my sick-bed I languish,
> Full of sorrow, full of anguish,
> Fainting, gasping, trembling, crying,
> Panting, groaning, speechless, dying.
> . . . . . .
> Methinks I hear some gentle spirit say
> Be not fearful, come away."

In the month of December, 1712, Mr. Pope wrote to Steele: "I do not send you word I will do, but have already done, the thing you desire of me. You have it (as Cowley calls it) just warm from the brain. It came to me the first moment I waked this morning; yet you will see it was not so absolutely inspiration but that I had in my head not only the verses of Adrian, but the fine fragment of Sappho." The thing Steele desired of him was " an Ode as of a cheerful dying spirit," and the result, in part, is here set down :—

> "Vital spark of Heavenly flame,
> Quit O quit this mortal frame;
> Trembling, hoping lingering, flying—
> Oh! the pain, the bliss of dying.
> . . . . . .
> Hark they whisper, Angels say—
> Sister Spirit come away."

What is known as "the deadly parallel" will prove that Pope's inspiration came rather from Flatman than from the original Sappho or from anybody else; and that the thing went to Steele not only warm from the brain of its doer, but warmed over!

Rare prints bearing the legend "*Faithorne Sculpsit*"—to return to the subject of portraits—have helped save from dull oblivion the counterfeit presentments of many better persons than Samuel Pepys's Lady Castlemaine; including Thomas Killigrew, 1644; Richard Hooker, 1662; Jeremy Taylor, 1663; John Milton, 1670; and Sir William Davenant, 1672-73.

From Jonson's inscription upon the portrait of Shakspere we turn, naturally, to the inscription under the portrait of Jonson, which was engraved by Robert Vaughan. It contains eight lines in Latin, and two in English, the latter reading as follows:

> "O could there be an art found out that might
> Produce his shape soe lively as to write."

In its first state, with the words "Are to be sould by William Peake," Mr. Chew believes that it was issued as a print. The second state was prefixed to the "Works," London, 1640, three years after Jonson received from King Charles I. eighteen inches of square ground in Westminster Abbey, and was left standing in his limited estate, in a grave "dug not far from Drayton's."

The lines on the Vaughan portrait are signed Ab. Holl.

"Ab. Holl" has been supposed to have been Abraham Holland, an intimate of Drayton whom he called his "Honest Father," and a friend of John Davies, of Hereford, who signed the inscription to the portrait of Captain John Smith, described below. Holland was the author of "A Resolution Against Death" and of a poem upon the Plague of 1625. He died, himself, despite his Resolution, in 1626; and, naturally, he could not have written the lines placed under a posthumous portrait of Jonson, who lived until 1637.

Bryan, who gives but few dates, says that "Vaughan died towards 1667." His latest plate, according to Horace Walpole, was executed in 1665. Vaughan's portraits are valued less for their merit as works of art than for the fame of their subjects. His print of Sir Walter Raleigh has a Latin motto above the portrait, and a three-line inscription beneath.

Marshall engraved a portrait of Jonson, "a laureated bust," which appeared on the frontispiece to "Horace," published in 1640. It was "printed for John Benson." Ben Jonson for John Benson is good!

A portrait of Jonson by William Elder, "with ten lines within the measure," was in the edition of the "Works" dated 1692. This is simply an enlarged copy of the Vaughan print, with the same Latin and English inscriptions.

William Elder was a Scotchman, who went to London about 1680. His portriats are not very many, nor do they represent a very distinguished list of names.

It is not generally known, by the way, that on the square stone which covers the top of the head of Jonson's upright figure in the north aisle of the nave of the Abbey, his name is spelled with the "h" —"O Rare Ben Johnson."

Richard Brome, who died in 1652, according to the author of the "Biographia Dramatica," "wrote himself into high repute, although his extraction was mean, he having originally been no better than a menial servant to the celebrated Ben Jonson." His quondam master addressed to him some complimentary lines on account of his comedy called "The Northern Lass," which was acted at the Globe and at the Blackfriars, and was published in 1632; and one A. B. signed the six lines at the bottom of the portrait, which appeared in the volumes of "Five New Plays," printed in 1653-59:

"Reader, lo here thou wilt two faces finde,
 One of the body, t'other of the minde;
 This by the Graver so, that with much strife
 Wee think BROME dead, hee's drawn so to the life.
 That by 's owne pen's done so ingeniously
 That who reads it, must think hee nere shall dy.
                                                "A. B."

This "A. B." is, no doubt, Alexander Brome (1620–1666), who wrote one comedy of his own, and edited the ten comedies of Richard Brome, published after the latter's death. He was an attorney in the Lord Mayor's Court, according to Langbaine, an enthusiastic Cavalier during the Civil Wars and the Protectorate; and he was given to the composition of odes, sonnets, dithyrambs, songs, and epigrams, all directed against the Roundheads and the "Rump." His relationship to his better-known namesake — known better, however, through Alexander's own exertions only—was not one of blood, but of brains. They were the fruits of two very distinct family trees.

Another writer of that, and a later period, whose verse did much to strengthen the Royal Cause after the Restoration, was Thomas D'Urfey, better known as "Tom." He lived until 1723; a contemporary of the Bromes, and a survivor of Addison, who helped him in his old age, on the ground that D'Urfey had written more odes than Horace, about four times as many comedies as Terence, and had "enriched our language with a multitude of rhymes, and bringing words together, that without his good offices would never have been acquainted with one another so long as it had been a tongue." He was a diverting companion and a voluminous writer, but not one of the thirty or more "dramatic pieces" of D'Urfey enumerated in the "Biographia Dramatica" were "on the muster-roll of acting plays" when that useful book was compiled, about half a century after his death; and Bartlett dismisses him, in a foot-note, as the author of a single Familiar Quotation—"Over the hills and far away." His collection of songs, satires, and irregular odes, published in 1719 under the quaint title, "Wit and Mirth, or Pills to Purge Melancholy," contains a portrait by George Vertue, and these three lines:

> "Whilst D'Urfey's voice his verse dos raise
> When D'Urfey sings his Tunefull Layes
> Give D'Urfey's Lyric-Muse the Bayes."

Although neither history nor tradition contains any account of intimate association between D'Urfey and Edward Ward (1667-1731), the author of "The London Spy," the simple fact that they were contemporaries, in London, that the one was a frequenter of taverns and the other a keeper of taverns, and the significant fact that each is still called, even at the end of two hundred years, by a familiar abbreviation of his first name, "Tom" or "Ned," would go to prove that they were both good fellows, and that they *must* have known each other. Giles Jacob, in his "Poetical Register," said that "Ned" Ward "kept a public house in the city, but in a genteel way;" and "Tom" D'Urfey was nothing if not genteel.

The inscription under Ward's portrait, engraved by Michael Vander Gucht, and printed in the first edition of his "Nuptial Dialogues," London, 1710—the title is significant—is expressed in the first person, it was evidently written by Ward himself, and it would seem to imply domestic relations which were somewhat strained. There can be little doubt, from the tone of the four lines, that "Ned" was generally spoken to, and spoken of, by the person of his house, as "Mr. Ward," or as "Edward." Thus they read:—

"Grant me O Hea'n! Good Humor still to please
My Wife, so long as she consults my Ease.
But give me courage, if she proves a Shrew
To scorn what none could ever yet subdue."

Michael Vander Gucht spent some time in London, and died there in 1725, at the age of sixty-six. He was the master of George Vertue between 1702 and 1709, and the author of many engraved heads, including those of Daniel Defoe, 1706; William Congreve, 1719; and John Aubrey, 1719.

Ward died in Fulwood's Rents, High Holborn, and was buried in Old St. Pancras Church-yard, in the most quiet manner. According to the directions of his poetic will no costly funeral did his executors prepare. 'Twixt sun and sun his only crave was a hearse and one black coach to bear his wife and children to his grave. This seems to show that Mistress Ward survived her husband, and consulted her own case in paying him the final earthly honors.

Aubrey said that Suckling (1608-1641) was "an extra-ordinarily accomplished gentleman, who grew famous at Court for his readie sparkling witt, as being uncommon readie at repartying, and as the greatest gallant of his time. He was of middle stature," Aubrey added, "and of slight strength, brisque eye, reddish fac't, and red nose (ill liver), his head not very big, his hayre a kind of sand colour;" and, still according to Aubrey, "he died a batchelor in Paris, and of Poyson, at the age of twenty-eight." Suckling, it will be remembered, was the author of "A Ballad upon a Wedding," containing the familiar lines: "Her feet beneath her petticoat, Like little mice stole in and out," etc.

Marshall engraved for the "Fragmenta Aurea," London, 1646, a portrait of Suckling in which no perceptible effect of the subject's ill liver, touched upon so delicately by Aubrey, is apparent. The eight lines at the foot of the picture prove that their author did not fear the effects of ill lights upon his forme.

> "SUCKLIN whose numbers could invite
> Alike to wonder and delight
> And with new spirit did inspire
> The THESPIAN Scene and Delphick Lyre;
> Is thus exprest in either part
> Above the humble reach of art;
> Drawne by the Pencill here you find
> His Forme, by his owne Pen his mind."

The portrait of John Smith, alluded to above, contains one of the earliest inscriptions in Mr. Chew's collection; it is dated 1616, and it is signed by John Davies.

> "These are the Lines that shew thy Face, but those
> That shew thy Grace and Glory brighter bee;
> Thy Faire Discoveries and Foule Overthrowes
> Of Salvages much Civilliz'd by thee

> Best shew thy Spirit; and to Glory Wyn,
> So, thou art Brasse without but Golde within
> If so; in Brasse (too soft Smith's Acts to beare)
> I fix thy fame, to make Brasse Steele out weare
> Thine, as thou art Virtues
> John Davies, Heref."

John Davies, of Hereford, the epigrammatist, was a writing-master and a poet: a writing-master to Henry, Prince of Wales, and a poet, although not a crowned laureate, to King James I. He lived among the wits and the players of his generation, Jonson, Bacon, Drayton, Sidney, Beaumont, and Fletcher; and he compared Shakspere to Terence, in his "Scourge of Folly," undated but published before Shakspere died, and long before Shakspere was recognized as the Immortal even by his own intimates. This is one of the earliest printed tributes to the Immortal now in existence: but as it was not inscribed upon a portrait, it has no place here.

In his reference to Captain Smith as being Brasse without, and in remarking that Brasse, as a rule, is too soft a substance to bear Captain Smith's various Acts, Mr. Davies, of Hereford, was, perhaps, epigrammatic, perhaps sarcastic, and perhaps he intended to be facetious. These lines were written some eight years before the appearance of the "Generall Historie," and, of course, before the writing-master could have read Captain Smith's vivid picture of one of his much civilized Salvages caught in the act of slaying, powdering, and eating his—the Salvage's —own wife: "Now, whether she was better roasted, boyled or carbonaded, I know not," saith the early and trustworthy historian of Virginia, New England, and the Summer Isles, "but of such a dish as poudered wife I never heard of." This playful allusion to powdered wife, and this serious speculation as to how she were best cooked, Mr. Charles Dudley Warner considers the first recorded instance of what is called "American Humor;" and he claims for Captain Smith, therefore, the honor of having been the first of the "American Humorists"—the quotation-marks are Mr. Warner's own—who have handled subjects of this kind with such pleasing gayety!

Mr. Granger and the later editors of

his great work were not very diffuse in their historical or chronological notes upon the British Heads they catalogued and described. The Jonson inscription under the Droeshout Shakspere is almost the only thing of its kind the work reproduces; and nowhere is any mention made of this 1616 portrait of Captain Smith. The earliest print of the founder of the multitudinous name, noticed in Granger, is that in the "History of Virginia," with the date 1632; and he referred to "a portrait by W. Richardson with six English verses," although he did not give its date, nor any hint as to where it first appeared. Walpole, however, said that Pass, probably Simon Pass, engraved a portrait of Smith in 1617.

Pass was born in Utrecht, in 1591. He is known to have spent about ten years in England, his earliest work there, according to Walpole, being dated 1613.

The portrait-inscription, in Mr. Chew's collection, next to that of Smith in point of antiquity, is addressed to Lancelot Andrews (1555–1626), and is dated 1618. The engraver is not known. The picture represents the learned prelate in cap and gown, and the lines are signed Ge: Wi: (George Wither).

> "These LINEAMENTS of Art, have well set forth
> Some outward features (though no inward worth),
> But to these LINES his WRITINGS added, cann
> Make up the faire resemblance of a MAN.
> For as the BODIE's forme is figured here
> So there the beautyes of his SOULE appeare,
> WHICH I had praised; but that in THIS place
> To praise THEM, were to praise HIM to his FACE.
> "GE: WI:"

Lancelot Andrews was successively Bishop of Chichester, Ely, and Winchester; and he should have been Archbishop of Canterbury. Bishop Hackett, his biographer, said of him that "the ointment of his name was sweeter than spices"; and Fuller, the biographer of almost everybody, remarked that "Andrews was so skilled in all, that the world wanted learning to know how learnèd he was." What George Wither thought of him, as on his portrait inscribed, has been shown above.

There are several portraits of Wither with laudatory verses attached. The earliest, engraved by William Holle, or Hole, was in "Abuses Stript and Whipt," London, 1615; and is one year earlier than the portrait of Smith. It exhibits the poet as very handsomely attired in rich slashed doublet, broad lace collar, and with a jewelled sword; and it represents him rather as a frequenter of courts than as the man who "lashed the follies of the time." It bears the legend, "G. W. anº Ætatis sua 21, 1611. I grow and wither both together," and has these six lines, signed Sʳ· T I. :

"Loe this is he whose infant Muse began
To brave th' World before years stil'd him man,
Though praise be slight, and scorns to make his Rymes
Begg favors or opinion of the Tymes;
Yet few by good men have been more approv'd,
None so unseene so generally loved."

No man of any distinction in England during the reign of the First James, either as a poet or as a patron of poets, bore these initials. And it is not known now who this "Sir T I" was.

William Holle, or Hole, flourished between the years 1600 and 1630. Very little is recorded concerning him, except that he was the earliest engraver of music on copper-plate in England, and that he was the author of heads of John Florio, 1613; Chapman, 1616; and Drayton, 1619.

The print of Wither, by Francis Delaram, with the date 1622, has the following lines:

"No matter wher the WORLD bestowes her PRAISE,
Or whom she crownes w'th her victorious Bayes.
For HE that fearelesse hath oppos'd the CRYMES,
And checkt the GYANT-VICES of the TYMES:
HE that unchanged, hath AFFLICTIONS borne,
That smiles on WANTS; that laughs CONTEMPTS to Scorne;
And hath most COURAGE where most PERILLS are,
Is HE that should of right the LAURELLE weare."

Francis Delaram lived in the reigns of Elizabeth and her successor. He is the author of portraits of Elizabeth, Henry Prince of Wales, and Charles [I.] Prince of Wales; and of a familiar print of "Will Sommers King Heneryes Jester [VIII.], after Holbein."

A third tribute to Wither was printed under the portrait by I. P. [John Payne] in the 1635 edition of the "Emblems":

"What I was is passed by,
What I am away doth flie,
What I shall bee none do see,
Yet in that my Beauties bee."

John Payne, a pupil of Simon Pass, was one of the earliest of the native English engravers of distinction. Evelyn spoke highly of him, and Walpole said, "The head of Dr. Alabaster I have [by Payne]; and it truly deserves encomium; being executed with great force, and in a more manly style than the works of his master."

George Wither (1588–1667) was a most voluminous writer. Allibone gave a list of nearly an hundred of his published works, in prose and in verse. He is believed to have been the original author of the idea that "care will kill a cat"— which care has never yet succeeded in doing—and it was his poetical shepherd who could not understand why he—the shepherd—should waste in despair and die, because a fair woman preferred to be fair not to him but to somebody else.

Charles Lamb in a letter to Southey, written in 1798, said: "I perfectly agree with your opinion of old Wither; Quarles is a wittier writer, but Wither lays most hold of the heart. Quarles thinks of his audience when he lectures; Wither soliloquizes in company from a full heart."

This, of course, refers to Francis Quarles (1592-1644). Marshall's portrait of Quarles was engraved for "Solomon's Recantation," London, 1645. Under four Latin lines, Alexander Ross (1590-1654), chaplain to Charles I., the Royal Martyr for whom Quarles suffered martyrdom, wrote:

"What here wee see is but a Graven face,
  Onely the SHADDOW of that brittle case
  Wherein were treasur'd up those Gemms, which he
  Hath left behind him to Posteritie.
                             "AL. ROSS."

John Quarles (1624-1665), the offspring of old smooth Francis Quarles, does not seem to have been born a very great poet, although Granger declared him "to have been the poetical, as well as the natural, son of his Father." He was, at all events, a good royalist, who suffered in the cause of his king; and he died of the Plague, and in poverty.

Thomas May (1595-1650) wrote for Marshall's portrait of John Quarles, to be found in the 1648 edition of "Fons Lachrymarum," the following inscription:

"But for his Face the Work had clearly gone
  For old smooth Quarles himself, and not his Sonne;

Who sighing how Kings fell, and Subjects rose,
Scornes to mis-spend one single Teare in Prose.
This Book's his shadowe, Hee's his Father's Shade
Quarles is a Poet as well Borne as made.
"T. M."

May, the eulogist, was a better rhymester, if not a better character, than the subject of his present verse. John Aubrey pictured him as a "Handsome man, debauch'd; lodged in the little square by Cannon Row, as you go through the Alley"; and Thomas Fuller asserted that "he was an elegant poet and translated Lucan into English." In early life he attached himself to the royalist cause, but tradition asserts that he expected to succeed Jonson in the laureateship, and that when Davenant received the appointment May changed his politics, and thenceforth warmly supported the other side. He wrote a prose "History of the Long Parliament" and several plays, in verse. Tradition further says that he became very stout in his later years, and that he was accidentally strangled to death in his bed by the strings of his own night-cap!

Thomas Fuller (1608–1661), more than once quoted here, was the author of a very entertaining "History of the Worthies of England," published in 1662, after his death. It is full of gossipy anecdote, and, with John Aubrey's "Lives of Eminent Persons," it is the basis of much of the existing biography of the Men of his Time. His memory is said to have been marvellous, even if it was not always to be relied upon. The earliest portrait of Fuller is to be found in "Abel Redevivus, or the Dead yet Speaking," London, 1651. It is not signed, but from the fact that the engraved title bears the name of Vaughan, and because the style of the portrait is very like that of Vaughan, there is little doubt, in Mr. Chew's opinion, that Vaughan is its engraver. There are no verses attached to it.

Two portraits of Fuller, each having four-line inscriptions at the foot, are familiar to the collectors. The first, by an unknown engraver, was printed in the "Life," London, 1661, and reads as follows:

"Nature t' expresse the Symetry of Parts,
Made this faire bulke the Magazine of Arts:
Body and Minde doe answer well his NAME
FULLER, Comparative to 's BLISSE and Fame."

The second, engraved by David Loggan, was in the 1662 edition of the "Worthies." It also plays upon the subject's name:

> "The Graver here hath well thy Face design'd
> But no hand Fuller can expresse thy Mind.
> For that a Resurrection gives to those
> Whom silent Monuments did long enclose."

David Loggan was born at Dantzic, in 1635. He studied under Simon Pass, and settled in England before the Restoration. He engraved a portrait of Alexander Brome, 1664; and two of Isaac Barrow, the first dated 1683. Loggan died, according to varying accounts, in 1693 or in 1700.

A contemporary of Loggan, and like Loggan an engraver imported into England, was F. H. Van Hove, who is described as having been "Dutch and prolific." He has left portraits of Bacon; Sir Thomas Browne, 1672; and William Winstanley, 1687. The dates of his plates cover a long period of time—from 1648 to 1692—and not the least rare of them bears the head of Edward Cocker, with this inscription:

"Cocker who in fair writing did excell
And in Arithmetick perform'd as well,
This necessary Work took next in hand
That *Englishmen* might *English* understand."

It is not positively known now in which of Cocker's works this portrait appeared. Besides writing his "Arithmetick," first published in 1654, which, according to Lowndes, saw upward of sixty editions, Cocker was a writing-master of great repute, and the author of many treatises upon this subject. Some of his quaint titles are worth recording. His "Copy Book of Fair Writing" appeared in 1657; the "Penna Volans," in 1661; "England's Penman," in 1671; "Cocker's Urania, or the Scholar's Delight in Writing," bears no date; and in 1675 he published "Cocker's Morals; or the Muses—a Book of Sentences for Writing," etc. It is said that Cocker engraved many of his "copy-books" on silver plates and with his own hand. The above verses in all probability were attached to a portrait in some one, or more, of these volumes. The following verses, no doubt, were under a portrait in one of the many editions of the "Arithmetick":

"Ingenious Cocker, now to rest thou'rt gone
No art can shew thee fully but thine own.
Thy rare Arithmetick alone can show
Th' vast sums of Thanks we for thy Labours owe."

Edward Cocker—"According-to-Cocker" Cocker (1631–1677)—was, according to Edward Hatton, "a person well skilled in all the parts of arithmetic. He was also the most eminent composer and engraver of letters, knots and flourishes in his time." He was, too, a collector of books and manuscripts; and, no doubt, a collector of the Inscribed Portraits of the men who flourished when he flourished himself. On the 10th of August, 1664, Pepys wrote "Abroad to find out one to engrave my tables upon my new sliding rule with silver plates.... So I got Cocker the famous writing-master to do it, and I sat an hour by him to see him design it all; and strange it is to see him, with his natural eyes, to cut so small at his first designing it, and read it all over, without any missing, when for my life, I could not with my best skill, read one word or letter of it; but it is use.... I find the fellow, by his discourse, very ingenious; and among other things a great admirer of, and well read in, the English poets, and undertakes to judge of them all, and that not impertinently."

Cocker's "Vulgar Arithmetick" was the strange gift of Dr. Johnson to his landlady's daughter at Anach. "Several ladies," wrote Mr. Boswell, "wishing to learn the kind of reading which the great and good Dr. Johnson esteemed most fit for a young woman, desired to know what book he had selected for this Highland Nymph. . . . And what was this book? My reader prepare your features for merriment. It was Cocker's Arithmetick!"

According to Cocker himself, Cocker was fond of fire-water, for he wrote in "Cocker's Farewell to Brandy" this awful warning: "Here lys one dead by Brandy's mighty power." It is not recorded, however, that Brandy, or any other excess, was the cause of Cocker's taking off.

Few of the Worthies of England who flourished at the beginning of the seventeenth century are better known, and better liked, at the end of the nineteenth century than is George Herbert (1593-

1632). His Life was written by Izaak
Walton; Bacon dedicated to him certain
of his translations of the Psalms; Coleridge called him "that model of a man, a
gentleman and a clergyman;" he was the
only author whom Cowper, during his
melancholy, had any delight in reading;
and Dr. Holmes, in his tribute "To Whittier on his Seventieth Birthday," two centuries and a half after the author of "The
Church Porch" died, could give the good
Quaker poet of the present "so fervid, so
simple, so loving, so pure," no higher
praise than to liken him "to Holy George
Herbert, cut off from the Church." Thus
hath Holy George Herbert, undivorced
from the Church, lived through all these
generations! To paraphrase his own
verse his own "Sweet and virtuous soule,
like seasoned timber, never gives."

"The Effigies of Mr. George Herbert,"
engraved by John Sturt in an edition of
the "Temple," published in London in
1709, has this inscription :

"Behold an Orator Divinely sage,
The PROPHET and APOSTLE of that age.
View but his PORCH and TEMPLE, you shall see

The Body of Divine PHILOSOPHY.
Examine well the Lines of his dead face,
Therein you may discern Wisdom and Grace.
Now if the Shell so lovely doth appear,
How Orient was the Pearl Imprison'd here!"

John Sturt was born in 1658, and he died in poverty and neglect some seventy years later. He was fond of engraving the Lord's Prayer, certain of the Psalms, and all of the Ten Commandments in small compass, sometimes so small that they could not be read without the aid of a magnifying-glass. Among his subjects of a larger size was a portrait of John Bunyan, a writer easily visible to the naked eye.

Good Izaak Walton, who wrote the Life of John Donne (1576-1631), as well as of George Herbert, is the author of the eight lines to the former gentleman at the foot of Marshall's portrait of Donne, printed with the " Poems" in 1635:

"This was for Youth, Strength, mirth and wit that Time
  Most count their Golden Age; but 'twas not thine.
  Thine only was thy later years, so much refined
  From youth's Drosse, mirth and wit as thy pure mind
  Thought (like the Angels) nothing but the Praise
  Of thy Creator, as those last best Dayes.

Witness this Booke (thy Emblem) which begins
With Love; but endes, with Sighes and Teares for
Sins. "Is. Wa."

The portrait represents the future divine and poet at the age of eighteen. Hence the allusion to his youth and its "Drosse."

Vaughan engraved a portrait of "Abraham Cowley [1618–1667] at the age of thirteen," which contains six lines of English verse, and was prefixed to the first edition of "Poetical Blossoms," published in London in 1633, when Cowley was a pupil at Westminster School, and only fifteen years of age.

The Cowley inscription is unsigned.

"Reader when first thou shalt behold this Boyes
Picture, perhaps thou shalt think his writings toyes:
Wrong not our Cowley so; will nothing passe
But gravity with thee? Apollo was
Beardlesse himselfe, and for ought I can see
Cowley may youngest Sonne of Phœbus bee."

Another younger son of Phœbus, beardless as Cowley or Apollo, was Francis Hawkins, who before he was eight years of age translated from the language of France a book entitled "Youth's Behaviour; or Decency in Conversation Amongst Men; Composed in French by Grave Persons for the Use and Benefit of their Youth; now Newly Turned into English." The work was first printed when Francis was in his thirteenth year; and it saw nine editions in all. In his "Address to the Publick" the publisher of the second edition—1646—apologized for "the Style . . . wrought by an uncouth and rough File of one greene in years." The edition of 1654 contains a portrait of the youth—according to Granger, by John Payne—under which, with the title:—" Francis Hawkins about the Age of Ten Years," is this inscription:

"See here th' effigies of a Child whose witt
So far outstripps his years & ruder thronge
That at Ten years he doth teach youth what's fitt
For their behavour from a forraigne tongue."

Hawkins entered the Society of Jesus in 1662—he was born in 1628—and he is now entirely forgotten, save by the few collectors of such things who are fortunate enough to possess the rare portrait in question. The fact that John Hawkins, the father of Francis, was a translator from the Spanish and the Italian, may, perhaps, account, in a measure, for the precocity of the son in putting into English, in such very green years, the writings of certain of the French.

Still another youth who lisped in numbers as a child, and whose wit far outstripped his years, but who is by no means forgotten now, was John Milton (1608–1674). "When he went to schoole, when he was very young," said John Aubrey, "he studied very hard, and sate up very late, commonly till twelve or one o'clock at night, and his father ordered the mayde to sitt up for him, and in those years [ten] composed many copies of verses which might well become a riper age."

There are in existence several portraits of Milton as a child, but most of them are proleptic, and none of them are prefixed to the works published during his childhood, for the simple reason that he published no works until his epitaph to Shakspere was printed in the Folio of 1632, when its author was twenty-four years of age. The earliest engraved portrait of Milton is that by Marshall, which figures as a frontispiece in his juvenile "Poems," issued by Moseley in 1645. It must have been taken from a still earlier original painting, for it distinctly calls him a youth of twenty-four, and the four lines of Greek verse at the bottom seem to indicate that Milton himself did not altogether indorse it as a likeness. No other satisfactory portrait of him could have been known to the engraver; and none appears to have existed, although Milton was then thirty-seven years of age, and was living, and teaching school, in the Barbican, Aldersgate Street, on unpleasant terms with his first wife, and his first wife's relations. George Vertue knew of no likeness of Milton between this of Marshall's in 1645—with no English inscription—and "the front" engraved by Faithorne for the "History of Britain," published in 1670, when Milton was sixty-two.

Mr. Charles B. Foote is the fortunate possessor of Vertue's own copy of one of his engravings of Milton. Below the portrait, Vertue has written, " This was done from the original print, engraved by W. Faithorne," and on the back of the portrait in Vertue's handwriting, signed G. V., are the following remarks: " This picture of Milton was painted in oyl, and had been in the Family until the death of Milton's third wife who kept it with great regard. She lived to a great age and died at Nantwich, in Cheshire. This was bought by a Gent. who brought it to London and sold it to the Hon^{bl} Arthur Onslow, Speaker, from whence I engraved it."

Old Jacob Tonson printed a monumental folio edition of Milton's works, "adorned with sculptures," prefixed to which, in a handsome frame, was a beautiful portrait of Milton engraved by Robert White, and containing the celebrated verses by Dryden :

> "Three Poets in three distant Ages born,
> Greece, Italy and England, did adorn ;
> The First, in loftiness of thought surpas'd ;
> The Next in Majesty; in both the Last.
> The force of Nature cou'd no further goe ;
> To make a Third, she joyn'd the former two."

Tonson was so proud of this performance that when his portrait was painted by Kneller for the Kit-Kat Club he had himself represented with the volume under his arm. A copy of this Milton folio, in fine old English binding, has been presented to The Players by Mr. Samuel P. Avery.

Robert White was born in London in 1645, and, according to Walpole, he died in 1704, although some of his plates are said to bear a later date. He was a pupil of Loggan, and a successful and voluminous engraver of portraits. In the Grolier Exhibition were, among others, the following examples of his work: Baxter, 1667, and 1670; Herbert, 1670; Flatman, 1682; Bunyan, 1688; Pepys, 1688; and Jeremy Collier, 1701. Walpole said "Many of White's heads were taken by himself, by a black lead pencil on vellum. . . . Vertue thought them superior to his prints;" and Granger wrote that "he was never exceeded in the truth of his drawings."

A tablet containing Dryden's lines to Milton was placed, many years ago, upon the outer—Watling Street—wall of the church of All Hallows, Bread Street, which stood upon the site of the edifice (destroyed in the Great Fire) in which Milton was christened. When the second All Hallows Church was taken down, in 1878, the tablet was inserted in the west wall of Bow Church, where it is still to be seen of every passer-by.

To end at the beginning. Professor Lounsbury, the recognized authority upon the subject, says that there is but one authentic portrait of Chaucer in existence—that made by Occleve upon the margin of one of his own works; a colored drawing of the man he styled his Master and his Father. It was painted from memory, as Occleve confessed, and probably after Chaucer's death. Thomas Occleve, or Hoccleve, was a poet, and a Writer to the Privy Seal. He is supposed to have been born about 1370, and to have died about 1454; which would make him many years Chaucer's junior, and his survivor for more than half a century. The Occleve portrait is on Leaf No. 91 of Occleve's "De Regimine Principum," Harleian MS., 4866. Upon it, of course, every subsequent likeness of Chaucer is based. George Vertue engraved at least three portraits of Chaucer; the earliest, dated 1717, was for John Urry's first edition of the "Life and Works of Chaucer," published in 1721. It has no inscription. The second, also in folio, was engraved for Vertue's set of the English Poets. The head is an exact copy of the portrait made for Urry's edition, although the ornamental frames are entirely unlike. It contains the following verses, written by Occleve himself, to accompany his original sketch of the Master and the Father of them all; and, although the portrait is late, the inscription is the earliest on record :

> "Althogh hys lyf be queynt the resemblance
> Of hym hath in me so fresch loftynesse
> That to putte othir men in rembraunce
> Of hys psone I have here hys lykness
> So make to this ende in sothfastnesse
> That they $_y^t$ have of hym lost thought and mynde
> By thys peynture may ageyn hym fynde."

An octavo print of Chaucer by Vertue was issued in the edition of the Canterbury Tales, published by Dr. Morell, London, 1737.

George Vertue (1684-1756) is famous as an antiquary and a scholar, as well as an artist. He belonged to a generation later than that of Droeshout, Faithorne, and Marshall. He was the author of several literary works upon engravings, and collections of engravings; and his notes and memoranda concerning English art were purchased, after his death, by Walpole, and became the basis of the "Anecdotes of Painting." His powers of catching and preserving a likeness are said to have been great, and his prints, on that account, are of much value and interest. Walpole gave a list of them which covers many pages, and includes a series of seventeen English Poets—from this portrait of Chaucer down to John Dryden.

There are extant, and addressed to all sorts and conditions of men and women, Portrait Inscriptions enough to fill a volume of any of the various editions of the British Poets now so common on both sides of the Atlantic. Those that are given here are only a few specimens of this interesting and obsolete form of literature; taken, almost exclusively, from the Inscriptions attached to the Portraits of the British Worthies who have made

British Literature itself, not those who have made British Laws or British History.

The Poets of Britain and of America to-day who write in English, dedicate their books, in verse, to their friends, and inscribe their presentation copies, in verse, to their intimates; but they leave their portraits, in the frontispiece, to speak for themselves, even when they feel that somebody else must speak for their poetry. To quote the slang of the profession—they get their Advance Notices in some other way.

ON POETICAL DEDICATIONS

CHAPTER V

ON POETICAL DEDICATIONS

THE first of the British periodical essayists, and the father of all later contributors to English and American magazines, wrote in *The Tatler* on May 26, 1710, and from The Trumpet, in Sheer Lane, that "the ingenious Mr. Pinkethman, the comedian, had made him a high Compliment in a facetious Distich by way of Dedication to his endeavours." This distich, unfortunately, has not been preserved; but it gave to the editor of *The Tatler* an opportunity to discourse most wisely upon the "Difference betwixt ancient and modern Dedications":

"In olden Times," he wrote, "it was the Custom [for authors] to address their Works to some eminent for their Merit to Mankind, or particular Patronage of the Writers themselves, or Knowledge in the Matter of which they treated. Under these Regards it was a memorable Honour to both Parties, and a very agreeable Record of their Commerce with each other." "But," he added later, "vain Flourishes came into the World, with other barbarous Embellishments; and the Enumeration of Titles and great Actions in the Patrons themselves, or their Sires, are as foreign to the Matter in Hand as the Ornaments are in a Gothic Building."

And thus, for a page or two, the venerable gentleman, then known to the reading world as Mr. Isaac Bickerstaff, berated his contemporaries, the moderns, for the fulsomeness and unmeaningness of their dedications, in a volume which is inscribed to the Right Honorable William, Lord Cowper, Baron of Wingham, and is signed "My Lord, Your Lordship's Most Devoted, Most Obedient, and Most Humble Servant, Richard Steele"!

The history of the dedications of books goes back as far as the beginning of the history of books themselves. Among the ancients, concerning whom *The Tatler* wrote, dedications were little more than prefaces and introductions, and it was not until what *The Tatler* considered modern times that they became the pegs upon which the author hung the compliments he bestowed upon that particular "Patron" who was willing to pay most generously for his praises. It is a curious fact that the earliest printed addresses and inscriptions of the poets themselves were generally written in prose, although it was a prose which contained, as a rule, quite as much poetry as truth; and that of all the examples, ancient and modern, noted and quoted in Mr. Henry B. Wheatley's interesting volume entitled "The Dedications of Books," not more than half a dozen are in verse.

Horace dedicated his first Ode, his first Epistle, and his first Satire, in metre, to his friend and patron, Mæcenas:

> "Mæcenas, scion of a race
> Of kings, my fortune's crowning grace
> And constant stay."—(Book I., Ode I.)

And Catullus dedicated his poems to

Cornelius Nepos, in lines which Mr. Andrew Lang has put into English for Mr. Brander Matthews's "Ballads of Books," as reprinted here:

> "*Quoi dono lepidum novum libellum.*"
>
> "My little book, that's neat and new,
>   Fresh polished with dry pumice stone,
>   To whom, Cornelius, but to you
>   Shall *this* be sent, for you alone—
>   (Who used to praise my lines, my own)
>   Have dared in weighty volumes three
>   (What labors, Jove, what learning thine!)
>   To tell the tale of Italy,
>   And all the legend of our line.
>
> "So take, whate'er its worth may be,
>   My book,—but Lady and Queen of Song,
>   This one kind gift I crave of thee,
>   That it may live for ages long!"

This same Mr. Andrew Lang, after rescuing the "Book" of Catullus from the language in which it had lain dead during so many ages, dedicated his own "Books and Bookmen," at the end of nineteen hundred years, and in accents unknown in the days of Catullus, to this same Mr. Brander Matthews, who had found for his wandering papers a home and a publisher in States then unborn.

"You took my vagrom essays in,
    You found them shelter over sea;
Beyond the Atlantic's foam and din
You took my vagrom essays in!
    If any value there they win
    To you he owes them, not to me.
You took my vagrom essays in,
    You found them shelter over sea!"

In the mean time Mr. Lang himself was made the subject of a poetic epistle which, if not a dedication, is worth reprinting here. In his "Underwoods" Mr. Robert Louis Stevenson wrote:

"Dear Andrew, with the brindled hair,
Who glory to have thrown in air,
High over arm, the trembling reed,
By Ale and Kail, by Till and Tweed:
An equal craft of hand you show
The pen to guide, the fly to throw:
I count you happy starred; for God,
When He with inkpot and with rod
Endowed you, bade your fortune lead
Forever by the crooks of Tweed,
Forever by the woods of song
And lands that to the Muse belong;
Or if in peopled streets, or in
The abhorred pedantic sanhedrim,
It should be yours to wander, still
Airs of the morn, airs of the hill,
The plovery Forest and the seas
That break about the Hebrides,

Should follow over field and plain
And find you at the window pane;
And you again see hill and peel,
And the bright springs gush at your heel.
So went the fiat forth, and so
Garrulous like a brook you go,
With sound of happy mirth and sheen
Of daylight—whether by the green
You fare that moment, or the gray;
Whether you dwell in March or May;
Or whether treat of reels and rods
Or of the old unhappy gods:
Still like a brook your page has shone,
And your ink sings of Helicon."

To which Mr. Lang replied in the following lines:

"Dear Louis of the awful cheek,
  Who told you it was right to speak,
  Where all the world might hear and stare,
  Of other fellows' 'brindled hair?'
'Shadows we are,' the sophist knew—
Shadows—'and shadows we pursue.'
For this my Ghost shall chase your shadow
From Skerryvore to Colorado."

But to return to the gentlemen who even in Mr. Bickerstaff's time were styled the "ancients." Master Geoffrey Chaucer, the "Floure of Poetes throughout all Britain"—

"That nobly enterprysed
How that our Englisshe might fresshly be enued,"

while given to prologues, does not seem to have indulged himself in dedications, although at the *end* of the last book of "Troylus and Cryseyde" he thus addressed a brother of the pen:

> "O moral Gower, this boke I directe
> To the, and to the philosophical Strode,
> To vouchen-sauf, ther nede is, to correcte,
> Of youre benignites and zeles goode."

Gower returned the compliment in the first form of the "Confessio Amantis;" omitting the eulogy, however, in the second form.

Chaucer's editors on more than one occasion have supplied Chaucer's deficiencies in dedication, for William Wynne, Chief Clerk of the Kitchen to Henry VIII., and editor of the first edition of Chaucer's works (1532), inscribed his volume "to that most gracious Defencer of the Christen Faithe, his most dradde soveraygne lord;" and Dryden dedicated his version of the "Tales from Chaucer," in the beginning of the eighteenth century, to the Duchess of Ormond, in lines beginning,

"The bard who first adorn'd our native tongue,
Tuned to his British lyre this ancient song:
Which Homer might without a blush rehearse,
And leaves a doubtful palm in Virgil's verse;
He match'd their beauties, where they most excel;
Of love sung better, and of arms as well."

Spenser's Poetical Dedications, that to the Earl of Leicester, "late deceased," prefixed to his "Virgil's Gnatt" one of the "Complaints," published in 1591, and that to "Maister Philip Sidney" introducing "The Shepherd's Calender" have nothing in them which warrants their being reprinted here.

The fact that Samuel Page, of Corpus Christi College, Oxford, dedicated "The Loves of Amos and Lama"—not his "Alcilia," as Mr. Wheatley has it—to Izaak Walton, in 1619, is worthy of note, because at that time Walton was only twenty-six years of age, and was entirely unknown to the world except as the occupant of a linen-draper's shop, seven-feet-and-a-half long and five feet wide, in the Royal Bourse, in Cornhill. His first work, the "Life of Doctor Donne," was not published until 1640, and "The Compleat Angler" did not appear until 1653.

When Page wrote his lines to the humble sempster he little dreamed that on their account alone posterity would remember him. Here are his claims to immortality :

"TO MY APPROVED AND MUCH RESPECTED
FRIEND, IZ. WA.

"To thee, thou more than thrice belovéd friend,
  I too unworthy of so great a blisse,
These harsh-tun'd lines I here to thee commend,
  Thou being cause it is now as it is;
    For hadst thou held thy tongue by silence might
    These have been buried in oblivion's night.

" If they were pleasing, I would call them thine,
  And disavow my title to the verse;
But being bad, I needes must call them mine,
  No ill thing can be cloathéd in thy verse.
    Accept them then, and where I have offended
    Rase thou it out, and let it be amended."

Perhaps these are the verses which inspired the subject of them to write five-and-thirty years later that angling and poetry are somewhat alike—" Men are to be born so!" He must have been a good fellow even in his youth, this Izaak Walton, born so himself. " The Compleat Angler " was dedicated in prose " To the Right Worshipful John Offley, of Madely

Manor, in the County of Stafford, Esquire."

John Taylor, "the Water Poet," dedicated "Et Habeo, Et Careo, Et Curo, A Poem" (1621),

> "TO EVERYBODY:
> "Yet not to every Reader, doe I write
> But onley unto such as can Read right;
> And with impartial censures can declare,
> As they find things to judge them as they are."

The reader of early biographical literature cannot help being impressed with the fact that most of the British men of letters before the close of the Georgian era are chronicled as being the Father of something. Chaucer was the Father of English Poetry; Walton the Father of Angling; Richardson the Father of the British Novel; Granger the Father of Extra-illustration; Steele the Father of the British Essay; and now comes a Scottish bookseller who figures as the Father of the Circulating Library. Allan Ramsay began life as a wigmaker in Edinburgh. He wrote a second canto to "Christ's Kirk of the Grene," no less than two kings of Scotland claiming the authorship of the first; he was esteemed so highly by Hogarth that the twelve plates of "Hudibras" were dedicated to him in 1726, and he figures in these pages as the author of a Poetical Dedication to Josiah Burchet, Esq., prefixed to "The Gentle Shepherd," his own great work, and closing as follows:

> "May never care your blessings sowr,
> A'n may the Muses, ilka hour,
> Improve your mind, an' haunt your bow'r,
> I'm but a callan;
> Yet may I please you, while I'm your
> Devoted Allan."

Ramsay retired from his original profession of "skull-thatching," as he himself somewhere described it, in 1718 or 1719, and during the rest of a long life he either sold, loaned, or made books. He was intimate with Gay, admired of Pope, praised by Boswell, snubbed by Johnson, and, according to Sir Walter Scott, he was the lamp at which Burns lighted his torch.

While dedications are not always altogether pleasing to the persons to whom they are addressed, it is not often that their very abusiveness adds to the market value of the books which contain them, as in the case of Churchill's "Sermons on the Lord's Prayer." Among their reputed author's posthumous papers was found an unfinished dedication to William Warburton, Dean of Bristol and Bishop of Gloucester, the character of which inspired the publishers to give £250 sterling for the ten sermons to which it was prefixed, sermons so poor in themselves that they are generally believed to have been the work of a duller, but better, man than the writer of "The Rosciad." Whoever originally delivered the discourses, however, there can be no question as to the authorship of the dedication. It is written in a strain of terrible irony.

"To Doctor! Dean! Bishop! Glo'ster! and My Lord!
. . . . . .
Let not thy brain (as brains less potent might)
Dizzy, confounded, giddy with the height,
Turn round, and lose distinction, lose her skill
And wonted power of knowing good from ill,
Of sifting truth from falsehood, friends from foes;
Let Glo'ster well remember how he rose,
Nor turn his back on men who made him great;
Let him not, gorged with power, and drunk with state,
Forget what once he was though now so high,
How low, how mean, and full as poor as I."

The Bishop of Gloucester, gorged with power, lived fourteen or fifteen years after this, and must have found comfort in the fact that the publishers of the Sermons suffered as much in their pockets by the venture as he did in his feelings.

It is not possible here to quote, or even to enumerate, the Poetical Dedications of the men of modern times. In previous generations, but within the present century, Keats inscribed, in 1817, to Leigh Hunt the little volume of poems which had already been printed in Hunt's *Examiner;* and Tom Hood dedicated his "Hero and Leander" to Coleridge in 1828.

"It is not with a hope my feeble praise
 Can add one moment's honor to thy own,
 That with thy mighty name I grace these lays;
 I seek to glorify myself alone:
 For that some precious favor thou hast shown
 To my endeavor in a bygone time,
 And by this token I would have it known
 Thou art my friend, and friendly to my rhyme!
 It is my dear ambition now to climb
 Still higher in thy thought,—if my bold pen
 May thrust on contemplations more sublime,—
 But I am thirsty for thy praise, for when
 We gain applauses from the great in name
 We seem to be partakers of *their* fame."

Shelley's "Queen Mab," printed in 1813, was dedicated "To Harriet" in lines beginning:

> "Whose is the love that, gleaming through the world,
> Wards off the poisonous arrow of its scorn?
> Whose is the warm and partial praise,
> Virtue's most sweet reward?
>
> "Beneath whose looks did my reviving soul
> Riper in truth and virtuous daring grow?
> Whose eyes have I gazed fondly on,
> And loved mankind the more?
>
> "Harriet, on thine: thou wert my purer mind,
> Thou wert the inspiration of my song."

. . . .

Whether this was written to Harriet Grove, his first love, or to Harriet Westbrook, his first wife, the commentators have not been able to decide; but there is no doubt that the "Mary" to whom "Laon and Cythna" (The Revolt of Islam) was dedicated in 1818 was the Mary Godwin to whom he had then but lately been married. In it he says:

> "So now my summer task is ended, Mary,
> And I return to thee, mine own heart's home."

. . . .

Scott prefaced the different cantos of

"Marmion" with poetical letters to different friends; and Byron, in what he called "good, simple, savage verse," dedicated "Don Juan" to Southey.

> "Bob Southey! You're a poet—Poet-laureate,
> And representative of all the race,
> Although 'tis true that you turned out a Tory at
> Last—yours has lately been a common case."

Among the men of our own day, Bayard Taylor dedicated, in verse, his "Poems of Home and Travel" to George H. Boker, and his "Poems of the Orient" to Mr. Richard H. Stoddard; Mr. Stoddard inscribing to Boker his "Songs of Summer." Mr. Swinburne dedicated "Songs of the Springtide" to Edward John Trelawney; Mr. Whittier, "In War Times," to Samuel E. and Harriet W. Sewell, of Melrose; Longfellow, the "Ultima Thule," to G. W. G. (George W. Greene); John Forster, the "Life of Goldsmith," to Charles Dickens; and Owen Meredith, "The Wanderer," to J. F., in a long poem dated Florence, September 24, 1857.

"Susan Coolidge" dedicated her "Verses" (Boston, 1881)

"To J. H., & E. W. H."

"Nourished by peaceful suns and gracious dew,
Your sweet youth budded, and your sweet lives grew,
And all the world seemed rose-beset for you.

. . . .

"Only this leaf, a single petal flung,
One chord from a full harmony unsung,
May speak the life-long love that lacks a tongue."

"Vignettes in Rhyme," the first American edition of Mr. Austin Dobson's verses, was introduced to American readers by Mr. E. C. Stedman, to whom Mr. Dobson dedicated his second volume, entitled "At the Sign of the Lyre."

"No need to-day that we commend
This pinnace to your care, oh, friend!
You steered the bark that went before
Between the whirlpool and the shore,
So—though we want no pilot now—
We write your name upon the prow."

In like manner he dedicated his "Proverbs in Porcelain" to Mr. Frederick Locker-Lampson, who is, perhaps, his only contemporary rival in their own peculiar and delightful line.

"Is it to kindest friend I send
This nosegay gathered new?

Or is it more to critic sure—
To singer clear and true?
I know not which, indeed, nor need.
All three I find in you."

H. C. Bunner's "Airs from Arcady" are inscribed

"To BRANDER MATTHEWS: BY THE HEARTH.

"Take these, the gathered songs of striving years,
And many fledged and warmed beside your hearth;
Not for whatever they may have of worth—
A simpler tie, perchance, my work endears.

"With them this wish: that when your days shall close,
Life, a well-used and well-contented guest,
May gently press the hand I oft have pressed,
And leave you by Love's fire to calm repose."

Mr. Whittier's gift to his intimates of a privately printed volume of his recent verse is inscribed to "The poet and friend of poets," Mr. E. C. Stedman, with these lines:

"Poet, and friend of poets, if thy glass
Detects no flower in winter's tuft of grass,
Let this slight token of the debt I owe
Outlive for thee December's frozen day,
And, like the arbutus budding under snow,
Take bloom and fragrance from some morn of May,
When he who gives it shall have gone the way
Where faith shall see and reverent trust shall know."

Lowell, by his own fireside, talked to Mr. Charles Eliot Norton, in "Under the Willows," of old times and of old scenes.

> "I sit and I dream that I hear, as of yore,
> My Elmwood chimney's deep-throated roar.
> If much be gone, there is much remains;
> By the embers of love I count my gains,
> You and yours with the best, till the old hope glows
> In the fanciful flame as I toast my toes."

Rather more tender is the dedication to "Among my Books."

> "To F. D. L."
>
> "Love comes and goes with music in his feet,
> And tunes young pulses to his roundelays;
> Love brings thee this: will it persuade thee, Sweet,
> That he turns proser when he comes and stays?"

These lines suggest Browning's "One Word More" at the conclusion of "Men and Women," inscribed

> "To E. B. B.
>
> "There they are, my fifty men and women,
> Naming me the fifty poems finished!
> Take them, love the book and me together:
> Where the heart lies, let the brain lie also."

To another good wife Mr. Aldrich dedicated "Flower and Thorn."

"To L. A.

"Take them and keep them,
Silvery thorn and flower,
Plucked just at random
In the rosy weather—
Snowdrops and pansies,
Sprigs of wayside heather,
And five-leaved wild rose
Dead within an hour.

"Take them and keep them:
Who can tell? some day, dear
(Though they be withered,
Flower and thorn and blossom),
Held for an instant
Up against thy bosom,
They might make December
Seem to thee like May, dear!"

And Professor Boyesen dedicated his "Idyls of Norway," in 1882,

"To L. K. B.

"I fain would praise thee with surpassing praise,
To whom my soul its first allegiance gave;
For thou art fair as thou art wise and brave,
And like the lily that with sweet amaze
Rocks on its lake and spreads its golden rays
Serenely to the sun and knows not why,
Thou spreadst the tranquil splendor of thine eye
Upon my heart and fillst the happy days,
Brimmed with the fragrance and the light of thee.

> Mute was my life and chill ere thee it found;
> Like dumbly heaving waves it rolled along
> In voiceless wrestling on a barren sea,
>   Until it broke with sudden rush of sound,
>   Upon thy sunny shore in light and song."

One of the most touching of dedications is that of Mr. James Whitcomb Riley, contained in his "Afterwhiles." It is very simple and very brief.

> "To HUMBOLDT RILEY.
> "I cannot say, and I will not say
> That he is dead—He is just away."

The Poetical Dedication to the book is what the prologue is to the play. They both serve to explain to the public the circumstances of the action of the work they introduce, or the situation in which the writer stands, or wishes to stand, in regard to the world at large. They address sometimes the whole audience of readers, but more often some one particular individual whose commerce with the author, as *The Tatler* quaintly puts it, is agreeable and affectionate, and an honor to them both. The score or so of poetical dedications given here, and the hundreds of others which must readily occur to the lover of books, will show, as emphatically as any other form of literature, the changes of thought and expression in English letters during the last five hundred years.

ON POETICAL INSCRIPTIONS

CHAPTER VI

ON POETICAL INSCRIPTIONS

QUITE as interesting as "Poetical Dedications," and much more valuable, because more rare, are those occasional autograph inscriptions in verse to be found on the flyleaves of certain printed books, but not originally intended to be printed themselves. They may be divided into three classes: first, those written by the author in the special copy of his own book which he has presented to his friend; second, those written by the recipient in the volume which his friend the author has presented to him; and third, those written in the books of men who are known neither to donor nor to recipient. They are fuller than marginal notes, and they are more personal and more spontaneous than dedications; they render the tomes in which they are contained absolutely unique, and sometimes they make a volume as precious to the collector of autographs as to the lover of books. A copy of "Venus and Adonis," for instance, in which Shakspere had written with his own hand,

> "Don't steale this Booke, my little Frend,
> For feare the Gallowes will be your end"

—if it existed—would be worth a mountain of First Folios of the Plays. There were only twenty-seven leaves in the little quarto volume in question, as first published in 1593, so the author could not have completed the inscription,

> "If you don't beleeve this Book is mine,
> Just turn to Page number ninety nine."

but as literature and as poetry the familiar quatrain is certainly as worthy of the author of "Venus and Adonis" as are the famous four lines carved upon the stone which is said to cover the dust and the bones enclosed in front of the altar of Holy Trinity Church at Stratford-on-Avon.

The Ancients, as *The Tatler* called them, were much given to writing sonnets to each other; but these were not always strictly personal—nor strictly true; and they always found their way into their authors' printed works, if not into the publications of the authors to whom they were addressed. Milton's famous "Epitaph upon the Admirable Dramatick Poet W. Shakspere"—"dear son of memory, great heir of fame," prefixed to the Second Folio Edition of Shakspere's plays (1632), and Wordsworth's "Sonnet to Milton," in the two volumes of "Poems by Wm. Wordsworth," first published in 1807, beginning,

"Milton! thou shouldst be living at this hour:
England hath need of thee," etc.,

are cases in point.

Among the earliest specimens of this complimentary verse are the lines addressed by Edmund Spenser to Gabriell Harvey, Doctor of Laws, printed in 1592, with "Foure Letters and Certaine Sonnettes Especially Touching Robert Greene, and Other Parties by him Abused." In an early edition of Captain John Smith's "History of Virginia" are prefixed almost a score of short poems—so called—the most notable, perhaps, being from the pen of John Donne; while, in 1616, George Wither congratulated his " Frend Captain Smyth upon his Description of New England," in harmonious numbers. Bengemennes Jonson wrote verses "to Master John Fletcher upon his Faithful Shepherdesse;" Fletcher wrote verses " To the True Master of his Art, B. Jonson," which are to be found in the edition of "Volpone the Foxe," printed in 1607. Beaumont wrote verses to Fletcher and Jonson, as Jonson and Fletcher both praised him ; and so each did laud the other, as all three of them eulogized, or were eulogized by, Nat. Field and by Chapman and by the rest of their contemporaries for pages.

On a blank leaf of a copy of Dugdale's "Monasticon," Warton wrote a sonnet, which is printed among his collected poems. Neither Warton nor Dugdale is remembered now. The former was Professor of Poetry at Oxford from 1757 to

1767, Camden Professor of Ancient History at the same university, and Poet-laureate of England from 1785 until he died in 1790, succeeding Whitehead, and immediately preceding Pye, in the long line of commonplace, half-forgotten versifiers who have held the office of Court Poet to the English kings. Sir William Dugdale was a distinguished antiquary in the seventeenth century; his "Monasticon Anglicanum" (1655-73)—a chronicle of the monastic and other foundations in England before the Reformation — has been placed next to the Doomsday Book itself as the most ancient and ample record of the history and descent of the greater portion of the landed property in the kingdom; and it has even been admitted as evidence in courts of justice when original titles and documents have been lost.

The lines written by Warton in Dugdale's great work, being comparatively unfamiliar even to the close students of English verse, and representing fairly the class of "poetry" to which they belong, are given here in full.

"Deem not devoid of elegance the Sage
By Fancy's genuine feelings unbeguiled,
Of painful Pedantry the poring child,
Who turns of these proud tomes th' historic page,
Now sunk by Time, and Henry's fierce rage.
Think'st thou the warbling Muses never smiled
On his lone hours? Ingenuous views engage
His thoughts, on themes, unclassic falsely styled,
Intent. While cloistered Piety displays
Her mouldering roll, the piercing eye explores
New manners, and the pomp of elder days,
Whence culls the pensive bard his pictured stores.
Nor rough nor barren are the winding ways
Of hoar Antiquity, but strewn with flowers."

Robert Burns, a contemporary of Warton, frequently expressed his affection for his friends upon the blank leaves of some favorite book before presenting the volume to the object of his regard. "Miss Cruikshanks," a maiden of twelve years, in whose father's house in Edinburgh he spent some time during the winter of 1787-88, was addressed by Burns as "Beauteous Rosebud, young and gay," on the page of a now-forgotten work; and on January 1, 1787, he gave a copy of Beattie's "Minstrel" to Miss Susan Logan, with the following lines:

"Again the silent wheels of time
   Their annual round have driv'n,

And you, though scarce in maiden prime,
    Are so much nearer heav'n.

"No gifts have I from India's coasts
    The infant year to hail;
I send you more than India boasts,
    In Edwin's simple tale.

"Our sex with guile and faithless love
    Is charged, perhaps too true;
But may, dear maid, each lover prove
    An Edwin still to you!"

Miss Logan was sister to the Major Logan to whom Burns addressed one of his "Epistles;" and "Edwin" is the hero of Beattie's poem.

Some fifty years later, in 1831 or 1832, Campbell sent a volume of his poems to his cousin Mary Sinclair, with the following inscription :

"Go, simple Book of Ballads, go
    From Eaton Street in Pimlico;
It is a gift my love to show—
            To Mary!

"And more its value to increase,
    I swear by all the gods of Greece
It cost a seven-shilling piece—
            My Mary!

"But what is gold, so bright that looks,
    Or all the coins of miser's nooks,
Compared to be in thy good books—
            My Mary!

"Now witness earth, and skies, and main!
The book to thee shall appertain;
I'll never ask it back again—
My Mary!

"But what, you say, shall you bestow?
For, as the world now goes, you know,
There always is a *quid pro quo*—
My Mary!

"I ask not twenty hundred kisses,
Nor smile the lover's heart that blesses,
As poets ask from other misses—
My Mary!

"I ask that till the day you die
You'll never pull my wig awry,
Nor ever quiz my poetrye—
My Mary!"

That our contemporary poets have been quite as happy in their Poetical Inscriptions as were the men of other days the verses which here follow will clearly prove. Many of these have never before been submitted to the public gaze, and such of them as are here printed for the first time are printed with the full consent of those to whom, or by whom, they are addressed.

An uncut copy of "The Virginians," first edition, was sold in London the other day with the following inscription, in Thackeray's handwriting, upon its fly-leaf:

"In the U. States and in the Queen's dominions
All people have a right to their opinions,
And many don't much relish 'The Virginians.'
Peruse my book, dear R.; and if you find it
A little to your taste, I hope you'll bind it.
Peter Rackham, Esqre., with the best regards
of the Author."

A copy of "Prince Lucifer" presented to Lord Tennyson contains these lines in the handwriting of Mr. Alfred Austin:

"Poet! In other lands, where spring no more
Fleets o'er the grass, nor in the thicket-side
Plays at being lost and laughs to be descried,
And blooms lie wilted on the orchard floor,
There the sweet birds that from the Attic shore
Across Ausonian breakers thither hied
Own that May's music in their breast hath died,
And sobering words resound not as before.
But in this privileged isle, this brave, this blest,
This deathless England, it seems always spring.
Though riper grow the days, Song takes not wing;
'Mid autumn boughs it builds another nest;
Even in the snows we lift our hearts and sing,
And still Your voice is heard above the rest."

As a Christmas greeting in 1876, Richard Henry Horne sent to Mrs. Henry Edwards an article of his own, contributed to an English magazine on the cover of which he had pasted an embossed card containing the following lines:

"Though age o'er garden, field, and tree
Must cast its thoughtful ash-gray shades,
   I send to thee
   O'er land and sea
A Rose of Love which never fades."

Although Mr. Frederick Locker-Lampson's library is wonderfully rich in autograph dedications and inscriptions, he gives but two examples in his "Catalogue," printed in 1886. These are four lines he himself wrote in a presentation copy of Dr. Holmes's "Songs of Many Seasons," and four verses written by Mr. William Morris in a copy of his "Love is Enough," addressed as follows:

"TO HANNAH JANE LAMPSON.

"Spring am I, too soft of heart
Much to speak ere I depart.
Ask the Summer-tide to prove
The abundance of my love.

"Summer, looked for long, am I;
Much shall change or e'er I die.
Prithee take it not amiss
Though I weary you with bliss.

"Laden Autumn here I stand,
Weak of heart and worn of hand.
Naught of rest seems good to me;
Say the word that sets me free.

> "I am Winter, that doth keep
> Longing safe amidst of sleep.
> Who shall say, if I were dead,
> What should be remembered?"

Beneath the inscription in Dr. Holmes's book, Mr. Locker-Lampson has written:

> "Some books are writ to sell—and don't!
> And some are read—such heavy tomes!
> But all should buy (though many won't)
> And read the books of Dr. Holmes."

In a copy of one of Mr. Locker-Lampson's own books, given by the author to Mr. Lang, he has written as follows:

> "By Enna's fold I strayed of yore,
> I've heard the pipe, I've plucked the wheat,
> And yet I would not give a straw
> To bide where any (Enna's) shepherds bleat.
> Give me in Shepherd's Bush a seat
> Where Pindar (classic Peter) sang,
> My *Daily News*, the vicious sheet
> Or pipe (if short!) of Andrew Lang!"

Mr. Edmund Gosse wrote in a copy of the "Hesperides" presented to Mr. Austin Dobson in 1878:

> "Fresh with all airs of woodland brooks
> And scents of showers,
> Take to your haunt of holy books
> This Saint of Flowers.

"When meadows burn with budding May,
    And heaven is blue,
Before thy shrine our prayers we say—
    Saint Robin true!

"Love crowned with thorns is on thy staff—
    Thorns of sweetbrier;
Thy benediction is a laugh;
    Birds are thy choir.

"Thy sacred robe of red and white
    Unction distils;
Thou hast a nimbus round thy head
    Of daffodils."

In the copy of "Letters to Dead Authors" presented to Mr. Brander Matthews, Mr. Lang wrote:

"Go, letters, to the irresponsive Ghosts
  That scarce will heed them less than living Men.
For now new Books come thicker than on Coasts
  And Meads of Asia throng the sea-birds when
The snow-wind drives them south in clamorous Hosts
  From their salt marshes by Cayster's Fen."

These lines, as an "Envoy," were subsequently printed in the second edition of the book.

Mr. Dobson about the same time put the following lines in a copy of his "Old World Idyls," addressed to an American friend:

"There is no 'mighty purpose' in this book,
Of that I warn you at the opening page,
Lest, haply, 'twixt the leaves you careless look,
And finding nothing to reform the age,
Fall with the rhyme and rhymer in a rage.
Let others prate of problems and of powers,
I bring but problems born of idle hours,
That, striving only after Art and Ease,
Have scarcely more of moral than the flowers,
And little else of mission than to please."

Mr. William Ernest Henley, the collaborator of Mr. Robert Louis Stevenson in the authorship of "Deacon Brodie" and other plays, is the possessor of a copy of "Dr. Jekyll and Mr. Hyde" in which Mr. Stevenson has written the following:

"Dramatic Jekyll and dramatic Hyde,
But which is which, let other men decide.
To the two friends, meanwhile, the work is fun,
And being never played, does harm to none."

In the copy of "The Paradox of Acting," presented by Mr. Walter Herries Pollock to a friend who disapproved of a Latin and later of a French prose inscription it contained, the author finally wrote:

"As no prose pleases, I must write in rhyme,
And wish the book were better worth your time."

In a paper upon Walter Savage Landor,

Lowell gave to the public not long ago a pair of quatrains he had written in a copy of Landor's works presented to a friend upon her marriage some years before. They are interesting as containing a condensation of the younger poet's judgment of the older.

> "A villa fair, with many a devious walk,
> Darkened with deathless laurel from the sun,
> Ample for troops of friends in mutual talk,
> Green Chartreuse for the reverie of one.
> Fixed here in marble, Rome and Athens gleam;
> Here is Arcadia, here Elysium too;
> Anon an English voice disturbs our dream,
> And Landor's self can Landor's spell undo."

In a copy of "Azarian," given to Mrs. T. B. Aldrich in 1866, Mrs. Harriet Prescott Spofford wrote:

> "Full often pictured on the page
>   Some reader sees a fair sweet face,
> That floats between the vacant lines
>   And paints the margin with its grace.
>
> "Precious because th' illumined sheet,
>   Though idle all its lettered lore,
> Here leaves a secret never sung,
>   And spells a charm unknown before.
>
> "Yet pages less fortunate than mine,
>   If here a fair sweet face shall bend,
> And to the trembling, happy leaf
>   Perchance one shade of beauty lend."

Mr. James Whitcomb Riley, having inadvertently written his name on the back instead of the front cover of a copy of "Afterwhiles," expressed himself thus in the proper place:

"LINES ON A ERROR.

"In the back of the book,
With his heels in the air,
You'll find your friend here,
Ef you look anywhere."

In a copy of Mr. E. C. Stedman's "Songs and Ballads," presented by Mr. H. C. Bunner to an intimate friend on the eve of that friend's marriage, Mr. Bunner wrote:

"The new year's not too old, my friend,
To wish a wish for you—
That the fire may ne'er grow cold, my friend,
That now shall shine for two;
The flame for kindly friendship set
Shall blaze for Love the higher yet,
Or be the heavens wintry wet,
Or summer blue."

Mr. Stedman possesses a copy of Crashaw's Poems, edition of 1670, in which Mr. Richard H. Stoddard had written in 1865 the following verse:

"To E. C. S.

"With a good long life
And a happy end,
These fine old songs
From his poor old friend
R. H. S."

On the same fly-leaf, in the handwriting of Mrs. Stoddard, is the inscription:

"My ornary powers
Allow but flowers.
'Tis for my bashaw
To send for Crashaw.
"E. D. B. S."

The following quaint lines are to be found in a copy of Miss Ellen Mackay Hutchinson's "Songs and Lyrics:"

"This little book it is so small
You scarce can call it book at all;
Yet prithee grant it so much grace
As on your shelf to keep its place,
This little book."

In a copy of "New Waggings from Old Tales," presented to Mr. Ernest D. North, Mr. John Kendrick Bangs, one of its authors, wrote the following lines:

"To E. D. N.

"If you ask for a garden with never a weed in,
Where bloom in profusion the flowers of readin',
Why, go you at once to the garden of E. D. N.

"To its master I send this small book of letters,
In the hopes that, if placed on a shelf with its betters,
When 'The Tales of the Wags' Mr. N. is perusing,
The wags of the Tales he'll not fall to abusing,
But ever continue his pleasant enthusing—
    Over me,
    J. K. B."

In a presentation copy of "Along the Shore," Mrs. Rose Hawthorne Lathrop has written:

"Is carking care a guest, and scowls the host,
  They dwell not there to whom I send thee:
Where cloud is least and hearty life is most,
  The H......' own the roof: to them commend me."

And in a presentation copy of "Gettysburg, a Battle Ode," are these lines by its author, George Parsons Lathrop:

"Dear kinsman H....., turn these leaves
  That in a chaplet I have bound
For those whose valiant suffering grieves,
  Though they our land with glory crowned,
And you will notice, while you turn,
  Our modern laurels are of paper,
Yet they at least, being good to burn,
  To light Fame's torch may serve as taper."

In the first copy of Mr. Eugene Field's "Echoes from the Sabine Farm," privately printed for Mr. Francis Wilson, Mr. Field wrote:

"This is a prize which cultured eyes
 Feeding upon do covet.
And well they may, I cannot say
 How very much I love it.
"That's why I send it to the friend
 Who favored me and brother.
Speed, pretty tome, into the home
 Of Wilson, and no other.
" He'll wonder what on earth he's got—
 'A birthday gift—a stunner.
Come, Mira, look! another book.
 And see! a number oner!'"

Unquestionably the worst specimen of this class of versification extant is the "Poem" written, by the author, in a copy of "The Curiosities of the American Stage," which he presented to Mr. Brander Matthews, to whom it was dedicated, in prose:

"This book to Brandar,
 Whose helping hand a
Lot did comfort and do me good.
Accept it Brandar,
 And understand a
Lot of gratitude understood."

These fly-leaves contain merely a sample of the unique treasures in this line which are to be found in the private libraries on both sides of the Atlantic at the present day. They are not only valuable in themselves, but they are of interest as showing the possibilities of Poetical Inscriptions, a form of literature to which the bibliophiles hitherto have paid but little attention. They show, too, that the knights of the pen have a fellow-feeling which is not always exhibited by the knights of the brush or by the knights of the chisel. While sculptors and painters rarely dedicate their works to each other, authors are very apt to inscribe to authors the books they write—a visible proof that the kinship of letters is more pleasant and more pronounced than are the personal amenities of pictorial and plastic art.

INDEX

Abbey, Edwin A., 4, 26
Addison, Joseph, 98
Adrian, 93
Alabaster, William, 109
Aldrich, Thomas Bailey, 26, 148-9
Aldrich, Mrs. Thomas Bailey, 148-9, 168
Allibone, S. Austin, 20, 109
Anderson, Alexander, 13, 14, 16
Andrews, Lancelot, 105-6
Arnold, Mathew, 25
Aubrey, John, 36, 100, 101, 102, 111, 112, 121
Austin, Alfred, 163
Avery, Samuel P., 124

Babington, Sir Anthony, 68
Bacon, Francis, 90, 103, 113, 117
Bacon, John, 55
Baker, J., 54
Bangs, John Kendrick, 170-1
Banks, Sir Joshua, 60
Barrett, Lawrence, 26
Barrow, Isaac, 113
Barry, James, 55
Bartlett, John, 98
Bartolozzi, Francesco, 6, 47, 69, 78

Baxter, Richard, 124
Beattie, James, 160, 161
Beaumont, Francis, 103, 158
Benson, John, 95-6
Bewick, Thomas, 6, 16
"Bickerstaff, Isaac," 132, 136
Blades, William, 39, 53
Blake, William, 47
Blount, Ed., 87
Boker, George H., 145
Bonaparte, Napoleon, 47
Booth, Edwin, 26
Bordone, Paris, 74
Boreman, Lady Dulcibella, 68-9
Boreman, Sir William, 68-9
Boswell, James, 35-6, 37, 50, 52-3, 54, 116, 141
Bowen, Abel, 17
Bowland, James, 25
Boydell, John, 69
Boyesen, Hjalmar Hjorth, 149-50
Boyesen, Mrs. H. H., 149-50
Bracquemond, Felix, 4
Brantôme, Peter Bourdelles, 79
Bretherton, C., 50-1
Brome, Alexander, 97-8, 113
Brome, Richard, 96-8

Browne, Sir Thomas, 113
Browning, Elizabeth Barrett, 148
Browning, Robert, 148
Bryan, Michael, 95
Buckingham, George Villiers, Duke of, 86
Bulwer, Edward Robert, Lord Lytton, 145
Bunner, H. C., 147, 169
Bunyan, John, 118, 124
Burchet, Josiah, 141
Burleigh, Robert (5th Lord), 74
Burleigh, William Cecil, Lord, 76
Burnet, John, 13, 14
Burns, Robert, 141, 160
Burton, John Hill, 37-8, 49, 50, 51-2
Bute, Marquis of (Lord Mountstuart), 37
Buttre, John, 51
Byrd, William (1st), 10-11
Byrd, William (2d), 11, 12
Byrd, William (3d), 11, 12
Byron, Lord, 145

Callender, Mr. (engraver), 13
Camden, William, 90
Campbell, Thomas, 161-2
Carlisle, Earl of, 65
Carwood, Amyas, 69
Cassellis, Earl of, 76-7
Castlemaine, Lady, 91, 94
Catullus, 133-4
Chalmers, George, 60
Chapman, George, 86, 108, 158

Charles I., 64, 66, 70, 76, 94, 108, 110
Charles II., 68
Charles IX. (of France), 64, 67
Chaucer, Geoffrey, 125-6, 127, 136-7, 140
Chew, Beverly, 14, 84, 94, 102, 105, 112
Childs, George W., 27
Churchill, Charles, 142-3
Clarendon, Edward Hyde, Earl of, 36
Clouet, François. (See Janet)
Cocker, Edward, 113-16
Colbert, Jean Baptist, 44
Coleridge, Samuel Taylor, 117, 143
Collier, Jeremy, 124
Congreve, William, 100
"Coolidge, Susan" (Sarah C. Woolsey), 145-6
Cornelius Nepos, 134
Cowley, Abraham, 93, 119
Cowper, William, 117
Cowper, William (Baron of Wingham), 132
Crashaw, Richard, 169-70
Critz, John de, 62
Croker, John Wilson, 52
Cruikshanks, Miss, 160
Curle, Barbara, 70-1
Curle, Elizabeth, 69-71
Curle, Gilbert, 70-1
Cure, Cornelius, 61-2
Cure, William, 62
Cushman, Charlotte, 20-1

Davenant, Sir Wm., 94, 111

Davies, John (of Hereford),
  95, 103-4
Dawkins, Henry, 13-14
Defoe, Daniel, 100
Delaram, Francis, 108
Denbigh, Earl of, 64
Dering, Thomas, 13
Dibdin, Thomas F., 38, 49,
  50, 51
Dickens, Charles, 145
Dobson, Austin, 146, 165-6,
  166-7
Donne, John, 86, 90, 118,
  138, 158
Doolittle, Amos, 13, 17-18
Douglas, George, 61
Douglas, Sir William, 61
Drayton, Michael, 90, 94,
  103, 108
Droeshout, John, 86
Droeshout, Martin (elder),
  86
Droeshout, Martin (younger), 83-91, 105, 127
Droeshout, Michael, 86
Dryden, John, 123, 124, 127,
  137-8
Duane, James, 106
Dugdale, Sir William, 158-60
Dunlap, William, 14
Durand, Asher B., 18
Dürer, Albert, 4, 5, 42
D'Urfey, Thomas, 98-100
Duyckinck, Evert A., 21
Duyckinck, George L., 21

Edwards, Mrs. Henry, 163-4
Eggleston, Edward, 27
Elder, William, 96

Elizabeth, Queen, 33, 62, 67,
  77, 108
Elliston, Robert, 12
Evelyn, John, 43-5, 91, 109
Everett, Edward, 19

Fairfax, George William, 88
Faithorne, William, 9 -2,
  93-4, 122-3, 127
Ferguson, Elizabeth Græm,
  21
Field, Eugene, 171-2
Field, Nathaniel, 158
Finden, E., 52, 54
Fiske, John, 4
Flatman, Thomas, 92-3, 124
Fletcher, John, 90, 103, 158
Florio, John, 108
Foote, Charles B., 122-3
Forster, John, 145
Francis I., 64, 74
Francis II., 64, 67, 75-6, 77,
  79
Francis, John W., 48, 50, 51
Franklin, Benjamin, 10
Franklin, John, 10
Fraser Tytler, Patrick, 66-7,
  76
Froude, James Anthony, 79
Fuller, Thomas, 36, 106, 111-
  13

Garrick, David, 27-8
Gay, John, 141
George I., 34
George III., 70
Godwin, Mary Wollstoncraft
  (Mrs. Shelley), 144
Goldsmith, Oliver, 145

Gordon, Watson, 72
Gosse, Edmund, 165-6
Gower, John, 137
Granger, James, 33-56, 104-5, 110, 120, 124, 140
Greene, George W., 145
Greene, Robert, 157
Greenwood, Mr., 37
Griswold, Rufus Wilmot, 21
Grove, Harriet, 144

Hackett, John, 106
Hall, H. B., 51
Halliwell-Phillips, James O., 85
Hamilton, James, Marquis of, 86
Harding, J., 55
Harvey, Gabriell, 157
Hatton, Edward, 115
Hawkins, Francis, 119-21
Hawkins, John, 120-21
Heath, J., 54, 55
Heere, Lucas de, 61
Henley, William Ernest, 167
Henry II. (of France), 64, 65
Henry III. (of France), 64
Henry VIII. (of England), 108, 137
Henry, Prince of Wales, 103, 108
Herbert, George, 116-18, 124
Herrick, Robert, 90
Herring, James, 51
Hoccleve, Thomas, 125-6
Hoey, Mrs. John, 48
Hogarth, William, 6, 141
Hogenberg, R., 43

Holbein, Hans (younger), 74, 108
Hole, William, 106-8
Holland, Abraham, 95
Holland, Henry, 43
Hollar, Wenceslaus, 47, 91
Holle, William, 106-8
Hollman, Julius, 51
Holmes, Oliver Wendell, 23-5, 117, 164, 165
Holt, Neville, 77
Hood, Thomas, 143
Hooker, Richard, 94
Horace, 98, 133
Horne, Richard Henry, 163-4
Howard, J. J., 19
Howson, John, 88
Hugo, Victor, 23
Humphrey, Ozias, 55
Hunt, Leigh, 143
Hurd, Nathaniel, 13, 22
Hutchinson, Ellen Mackay, 21, 170

Iaggard, Isaac, 87
Ingelow, Jean, 20
Ireland, Joseph Norton, 48, 50, 51

Jacob, Giles, 99
Jaggard, Isaac, 87
James I. and VI., 61, 68, 72, 76, 103, 107, 108
James II., 70
James V. (of Scotland), 78
Janet (François Clouet), 64-6, 77
Jehannet. (See Janet)

Johnson, Samuel, 35. 37, 52,
53-5, 116, 141
Johnson, Mrs. Samuel, 53
Jonson, Benjamin, 83-4, 87,
88, 90, 94-6, 103, 105, 111,
158

Keats, John, 143
Killigrew, Thomas, 94
Kneller, Geoffrey, 124
Knollies, Sir Francis. 78

Labanof, Prince. 67, 73
Lamb, Charles. 109
Lampson, Hannah Jane,
164-5
Lampson. (See Frederick
Locker)
Landor, Walter Savage,
167-8
Lang, Andrew. 20, 134-6,
165, 166
Langbaine, Gerard, 97
Langton, Bennet, 54
Langton, George, 52
Lathrop, George Parsons,
171
Lathrop, Rose Hawthorne,
171
Lawrence. Sir Thomas, 52
Lawrence, Thomas W., 56
Leicester, Earl of, 138
Lely, Peter, 91
Leslie, Frank. 48
Lichenstein, Richard C., 12,
14, 18-19
Locker-Lampson, Frederick, 146-7, 164-5
Logan, Major, 161

Logan, Susan, 160-1
Loggan, David, 113, 124
Longfellow, Henry W., 145
Louis XIV., 44
Lounsbury, Thomas R., 125
Lowell, James Russell, 148,
168
Lowndes, William Thomas,
114
Lucian, 111
Lytton - Bulwer, Edward
Robert, 145

Mæcenas, 133
Malone, Edmund, 54, 88
Marriot, Richard, 45
Marshall, William, 6, 89-90,
95, 102, 110, 118, 122, 127
Mary of Guise, 63-4, 78
Mary, Queen of Scots, 47,
50, 53, 59-79
Matthews, Brander, 26, 134,
147. 166, 172
Mauran, James Eddy, 18
Maverick, Peter. 13, 17. 18,
22
Maverick, Peter R., 13, 17,
18, 22
May, Thomas. 90, 110-11
Melville, Sir James, 77
Meres, Francis, 62
Milton, John, 94, 121-5, 157
Milton, Mrs. John (1st), 122
Milton, Mrs. John (3d), 123
Molière, 26
More, Sir Thomas. 90
Moreau, Charles C., 17, 56
Morell, Thomas, 126
Morris, William, 164

Morton, Earl of, 60-61
Moseley, Humphrey, 122
Mountstuart, Lord (Marquis of Bute), 37
Murray, John (2d), 53

Nanteuil, Robert, 44, 91
Napier, Lord, 63-4
Neil, P. G. J., 65
Nepos, Cornelius, 134
Noble, Mark, 34
Nollekins, Joseph, 55
North, Ernest D., 170-1
Northcote, James, 55
Norton, Charles Eliot, 148
Nottingham, Earl of, 43-4

Occleve, Thomas, 125-6
Offley, John, 139-40
Oliver, Isaac, 74
Onslow, Arthur, 123
Opie, John, 55
Orkney, Earl of, 72
Ormond, Duchess of, 137-8
Overbury, Sir Thomas, 86
"Owen Meredith," 145

Page, Samuel, 138-9
Parker, Matthew, 43
Pass, Simon, 105, 109, 113
Payne, John, 108-9, 120
Peake, William, 94
Pepys, Samuel, 43-5, 91, 94, 115-16, 124
Pepys, Mrs. Samuel, 44
Phillips, Thomas, 51
Pinkethman, William, 131
Pliny, 42
Pollock, Walter Herries, 167

Pope, Alexander, 14, 92-3, 141
Poulet-Malassis, A. P., 21, 22, 23
Prescott, William H., 19
Primevra, Jacopo, 75
Pye, Henry James, 159

Quarles, Francis, 90, 109-10
Quarles, John, 90, 110-11

Rackham, Peter, 163
Raleigh, Sir Walter, 95
Ramsay, Allan, 140-1
Revere, Paul, 13, 14-15, 16, 18
Reynolds, Frances, 55
Reynolds, Sir Joshua, 52, 53-5
Richardson, Jonathan, 41
Richardson, Samuel, 140
Richardson, W., 105
Riley, Humbolt, 150
Riley, James Whitcomb, 150, 169
Roget, Peter Mark, 24
Ross, Alexander, 110

Sage, Dean, 27
Sappho, 93
Scharf, George, 87-9
Scott, Sir Walter, 69-70, 141, 144-5
Scott, Winfield, 19
Seton, David, 73
Seton, Lord, 67
Seton, Mary, 78
Seton, William, 73
Sewell, Harriet W., 145

Sewell, Samuel E., 145
Shakspere, 47, 53, 83-91, 91, 103, 105, 121, 156, 157
Shelley, Harriet Westbrook, 144
Shelley, Mary Wollstoncraft Godwin, 144
Shelley, Percy Bysche, 144
Shirley, James, 90
Sidney, Sir Philip, 103, 138
Sinclair, Mary, 161-2
Smith, Captain John, 95, 102-5, 107, 158
Sommers, Will, 108
Southey, Robert, 109, 145
Speed, John, 49
Spenser, Edmund, 138, 157
Spofford, Harriet Prescott, 168
Stedman, Edmund Clarence, 21, 25, 146, 147, 169-70
Steele, Richard, 92-3, 131-2, 133, 140, 157
Stevenson, Robert Louis, 135-6, 167
Stewart, Mr., 67
Stoddard, Richard H., 145, 169-70
Stoddard, Mrs. R. H., 170
Strickland, Agnes, 69
Stuart, Mary, Queen of Scots, 47, 50, 53, 59-79
Stuart, Robert, Earl of Orkney, 72
Sturt, John, 117-18
Suckling, Sir John, 90, 101-2
Sutherland, Duke of, 54, 71
Swinburne, Algernon Chas., 145

Taylor, Bayard, 145
Taylor, Jeremy, 94
Taylor, John, 140
Taylor, Tom, 55
Tennyson, Alfred, 163
Terrence, 103
Thackeray, Wm. M., 162-3
Thomson, James, 51
Toedtberg, Augustus, 56
Tonson, Jacob, 14, 123-4
Tredwell, Daniel M., 39
Trelawney, Edward Chas., 145
Trent, George, 56
Trotter, S. C., 55
Turner, James, 13

Urry, John, 126

Vander Gucht, Michael, 100
Vandyck, Anthony, 74
Van Hove, F. H., 113
Varick, Richard, 16
Vaughan, Robert, 94-5, 96, 112
Vertue, George, 6, 42, 47, 74, 99, 100, 122-3, 124, 125-7
Victoria, Queen, 70, 76
Villiers, George, Duke of Buckingham, 86
Virgil, 138

Wallack, John Lester, 48
Walpole, Horace, 34-5, 36, 43, 60, 63, 67, 91, 95, 105, 109, 124, 127
Walton, Izaak, 36, 45-6, 90, 117, 118-19, 138-40
Warburton, William, 142-3

Ward, Edward, 99-101
Ward, Mrs. Edward, 100, 101
Warner, Charles Dudley, 104
Warton, Thomas, 158-60
Washington, Andrew, 8-9
Washington, George, 9, 16, 27, 47
Washington, John, 8-9
Watts, Isaac, 49
Webster, Daniel, 19
Welbrook, Harriet (Mrs. Shelley), 144
Wheatley, Henry B., 133, 138
White, Robert, 123, 124
Whitehead, William, 159
Whittier, John G., 117, 145, 147
Whyte, Nicholas, 76
Wilkie, Sir David, 71
Wingham, William Cowper, Baron of, 132
Wilson, Francis, 171-2
Winstanley, William, 113
Wither, George, 106-9, 158
Woolsey, Sarah C. ("Susan Coolidge"), 145-6
Wordsworth, William, 157
Wynne, William, 137

Zoffany, John, 55
Zuccaro, Frederigo, 67, 68, 74

THE END

By LAURENCE HUTTON.

LITERARY LANDMARKS OF LONDON. (*New Edition.*) Illustrated with over 70 Portraits. Post 8vo, Cloth, Ornamental, $1 75.

Altogether this is a book of which literary America may be proud and literary London ashamed. Mr. Hutton has done for us what we have never done for ourselves.—*Saturday Review*, London.

LITERARY LANDMARKS OF EDINBURGH. Illustrated. Post 8vo, Cloth, Ornamental, $1 00.

With marked skill Mr. Laurence Hutton has in this volume presented an endless amount of valuable information relative to the many illustrious men of letters who have lived in Edinburgh. He has hunted up tradition, verified the facts, as only a passionate pilgrim could, and we are grateful to him for the planting of these literary landmarks.—*N. Y. Times.*

CURIOSITIES OF THE AMERICAN STAGE. With Copious and Characteristic Illustrations. Crown 8vo, Cloth, Uncut Edges and Gilt Top, $2 50.

The work presents a mass of valuable information in a most attractive and readable form In it an admirable literary quality, seldom found in such histories, is conspicuous on every page, and the usually dry catalogue of names and dates is elevated from the plain of mere schedule by manifold touches of delicious humor, shrewd comment, and tender pathos.—*Christian Union*, N. Y.

Published by HARPER & BROTHERS, New York.

☞ *Any of the above works will be sent by* HARPER & BROTHERS, *postage prepaid, to any part of the United States, Canada, or Mexico, on receipt of the price.*

By WILLIAM DEAN HOWELLS.

THE QUALITY OF MERCY. 12mo, Cloth, $1 50.

AN IMPERATIVE DUTY. 12mo, Cloth, $1 00.

CRITICISM AND FICTION. With Portrait. 16mo, Cloth, Ornamental, $1 00.

THE ALBANY DEPOT. Illustrated. 16mo, Cloth, 50 cents.

A BOY'S TOWN. Illustrated. Post 8vo, Cloth, Ornamental, $1 25.

THE SHADOW OF A DREAM. 12mo, Cloth, $1 00 ; Paper, 50 cents.

A HAZARD OF NEW FORTUNES. 12mo, Cloth, 2 vols., $2 00 ; Illustrated, 12mo, Paper, $1 00.

ANNIE KILBURN. 12mo, Cloth, $1 50 ; Paper, 75 cents.

APRIL HOPES. 12mo, Cloth, $1 50 ; Paper, 75 cents.

THE MOUSE-TRAP, and Other Farces. Illustrated. 12mo, Cloth, $1 00.

MODERN ITALIAN POETS. Portraits. 12mo, Half Cloth, $2 00.

Published by HARPER & BROTHERS, New York.

☞ *Any of the above works will be sent by mail, postage prepaid, to any part of the United States, Canada, or Mexico, on receipt of the price.*

www.ingramcontent.com/pod-product-compliance
Lightning Source LLC
Chambersburg PA
CBHW020843160426
43192CB00007B/763